Teaching Off Trail

Teaching
Off Trail

My Classroom's Nature
Transformation
through Play

Peter
Dargatz

Redleaf Press®
www.redleafpress.org
800-423-8309

Published by Redleaf Press
10 Yorkton Court
St. Paul, MN 55117
www.redleafpress.org

First edition 2022

Cover design by Michelle Lee Lagerroos

Cover photographs, clockwise from top right: ©photophonie - stock.adobe.com; photo courtesy of the author; ©CandyRetriever - stock.adobe.com; iStock.com/ND1939; ©Andrey_Arkusha - stock.adobe.com; photos courtesy of the author

Interior design by Michelle Lee Lagerroos

Typeset in Museo Sans Rounded and Museo Slab

Interior photos: pages xiii and 4: ©Sergey Novikov - stock.adobe.com; page 16: ©Rawpixel.com - stock.adobe.com; page 19: ©photophonie - stock.adobe.com; page 28: Michelle Lee Lagerroos; page 49: ©Blue Planet Studio - stock.adobe.com; page 59: ©Robert Kneschke - stock.adobe.com; page 64: ©thepoo - stock.adobe.com; page 81: ©jessica - stock.adobe.com; page 82: Michelle Lee Lagerroos; page 83: ©micromonkey - stock.adobe.com; page 104: ©wuttichok - stock.adobe.com; page 107: ©Maria Sbytova - stock.adobe.com; page 122:© hakase420 - stock.adobe.com; page 131: Michelle Lee Lagerroos; page 142: ©pingpao - stock.adobe.com. All other photos courtesy of the author.

Chapter icons by ©glorcza - stock.adobe.com; ©LynxVector - stock.adobe.com; ©dlyastokiv - stock.adobe.com; ©bsd555 - stock.adobe.com; ©kadevo - stock.adobe.com; ©yudi - stock.adobe.com

Printed in the United States of America

28 27 26 25 24 23 22 21   1 2 3 4 5 6 7 8

Library of Congress Cataloging-in-Publication Data
Names: Dargatz, Peter, author.
Title: Teaching off trail : my classroom's nature transformation through play / by Peter Dargatz.
Description: First edition. | St. Paul, MN : Redleaf Press, 2022. | Includes bibliographical references and index. | Summary: "This book offers strategies for readers to implement the author's unique teaching philosophy to increase opportunities for play, creative expression, and personalization in both the indoor and outdoor classroom. In his own classroom, Peter brought learning outside by creating a nature kindergarten program that emphasizes community partnerships, service learning, and meaningful and memorable experiences in the outdoors. He incorporates techniques often identified as more informal settings like Reggio or Montessori, and shows how they work within a public school System"— Provided by publisher.
Identifiers: LCCN 2021026493 (print) | LCCN 2021026494 (ebook) | ISBN 9781605547503 (paperback) | ISBN 9781605547510 (ebook)
Subjects: LCSH: Outdoor education. | Play. | Early childhood education.
Classification: LCC LB1047 .D37 2022 (print) | LCC LB1047 (ebook) | DDC 371.3/84--dc23
LC record available at https://lccn.loc.gov/2021026493
LC ebook record available at https://lccn.loc.gov/2021026494

Printed on acid-free paper

To Embry, Oakley,
and Arden

My favorite tyke hikers
who make every day a
playful adventure

Contents

Foreword

If you're looking for a traditional foreword, you've come to the wrong place. This book is all about teaching off trail and playing with a purpose. With that, welcome to my game—I mean, book.

It's time for America's favorite educational game show, *Which Education Is Best?* Here is your host and author, Peterrrrrrrrrrrrrrrrrrrrrrrrrrrrrrrrrrrrr "Rhymes with Targets" Dargatz.

Good evening everyone! Welcome to *Which Education Is Best?* Wow, what a treat awaits you tonight: our championship finale and the answer to the question we've all been waiting for—Which education is best?

For centuries, philosophers, scientists, teachers, researchers, and even politicians have discussed and debated the best model for educating our youth, engendering progress and causing problems along the way. The time for discussion is over. It's time for action.

Tonight our two remaining teams will finally answer that age-old question. Say it with me!

Which education is best?

Let's meet our championship teams!

Dr. Rachel Larimore and Megan Gessler of Team Nature-Based have dominated their competition up to this point, dismantling Team Direct Instruction and squeaking out a victory over Team Experiential Learning on their way to the finals. Rachel and Megan, please introduce yourselves to those at home.

Rachel: I'm originally a farm kid from central Illinois, now living in Michigan. I'm a scholar, author, speaker, and consultant focused on nature-based early childhood education with my business, Samara Early Learning. Prior to this, I served for ten years as the founding director of a nature-based preschool, and before that I was a nonformal environmental educator for about twelve years.

Megan: Hello, fellow passionate educators! Much like Rachel, I too come from Illinois farmland. I spent much of my childhood summers camping around the country with my family and developing a love of nature. After having children of my own, I decided that our amazing family experiences with camping, scouting, and 4-H didn't go far enough in providing space for children to develop a kinship with nature, so I followed my heart and earned my master's in education at Antioch University New England, along with my Nature-Based Early Childhood Education Certificate. I have ten years of experience founding, directing, and teaching in nature-based preschools, and I am the founder of the Northern Illinois Nature Preschool Association. With our combined experience, Rachel and I make a formidable team!

Peter: Thanks Team Nature-Based! Let's meet your competition: Team Play-Based!

Fresh off the release of their amazing book, *The Playful Classroom*, Jed Dearybury ("DairyBerry") and Dr. Julie P. Jones are riding high after conquering Team Lecture and defeating Team Independent Study in overtime. Welcome back Julie and Jed! Tell us a little about yourselves.

Julie: Hey, y'all! While my favorite skill set is capturing literary criminals with a cup of hot tea beside me, my public role is equipping and empowering future teachers. I am director of student teaching and elementary education at Converse College in Spartanburg, South Carolina, and mommy to two middle-school-aged girls who tolerate my playful, imaginative spirit and keep me on my toes.

Jed: Hey, fabulous people reading this book! For almost two decades, I have been educating everyone from elementary to college kids (and their sometimes-boring professors) about the power of play for *all* ages. Our team is no doubt the best in this educational game show. My sparkle along with Julie's imaginative spirit makes for a great duo!

Peter: All right, teams. It's time to play *Which Education Is Best?* Round One is called *Buzz or Bust*. In this round, each contestant will be given a current educational buzzword and thirty seconds to explain how their type of education utilizes that word. Once both teams have finished their explanations, their opponents can choose to "bust" their buzzword. Let's get started!

Nature-Based, you're up first. Rachel, your buzzword is *informal assessment*. Your thirty seconds start now!

Rachel: Well, *informal assessment* is the ongoing observation of children to identify how they're developing physically, cognitively, socially, and emotionally. This type of assessment isn't a formal, sit-down test that every other child in the county, state, or country is taking. Instead, children are observed as they go about their daily lives of play. Rather than creating an artificial situation to "test" their knowledge or skills, we use authentic assessment to observe how they move their bodies, use language, write words, and so forth. In other words, we just pay attention! Now, I will say, I don't love the term *informal* because it makes the assessment process sound loosey-goosey or willy-nilly. Ongoing, authentic assessment *is* intentional — BZZZZZ!

Peter: And time! Play-Based, get ready! Julie, your buzzword is *social-emotional learning*. Your thirty seconds start now!

Julie: Oh, yes! When most people hear *social-emotional learning*, they think of weekly guidance lessons. Sadly, many educators still have a separatist view on this concept. But in the new integrated paradigm, cognition, emotions, and movement are not considered separate entities. We don't keep them in the tidy drawers of a brain cabinet. These aspects of ourselves are integrated, like a bowl of happy spaghetti, and that integration is beautiful! Our cognitive experiences become hardwired to our emotions and strengthened when movement is also present. Our brain remembers each experience through the emotions tied to it. Is it playful? We sure hope so! Social emotional learning *is* the learning.

Peter: And time! Back to Team Nature-Based and Megan. Your buzzword is *building empathy*. Your thirty seconds start now!

Megan: Sorry, I'm busy eating my bowl of happy spaghetti. Yum! What better way to explore empathy than in nature, where so many provocations abound! Children can observe similarities and differences between plants, learn how to care for animals by filling bird feeders or moving worms from the sidewalk to the soil, explore adaptation by observing how birds flock together for protection, notice the effects of predator-prey relationships, or witness the life cycle by examining remains—all of these experiences with other-than-human life forms lead to a more holistic understanding and feeling of kinship with all of nature, including humans. And now, I'm off to find the garlic bread—

Peter: And time! Here comes our final buzzword for round one; Jed, your word is *inclusion*. Your thirty seconds start now.

Jed: Playful learning and teaching absolutely level the field to make the classroom more inclusive. Playing destroys the rigid boxes that life often puts us into. Who needs to think outside the box, anyway? Just destroy it altogether. The confining walls of the boxes we live in often separate us into isolation. Playing literally tears down those barriers and brings us all together. Students, young and old alike, need time, space, and opportunity to experience those freeing moments that play provides. Go for it, y'all! You will be happier than a mule in a pickle patch! BZZZZZ!

Peter: What a whirlwind of a first round. But the game isn't over yet. It's time for round two—busting time! In this round, teams switch words and aim to bust the other team's reasoning to show why their method fits the needs of that buzzword even better.

Okay, Team Nature-Based, let's get busting! Rachel, please bust *social-emotional learning*.

Rachel: Oh, social-emotional learning is foundational to everything! Our internal emotions and social interactions with others are deeply connected to our development in other domains. Things like awe, wonder, curiosity, motivation, empathy, compassion, creativity, and persistence support children's physical and cognitive development. These skills, and so many more, are vital to children's livelihoods and growth. Play in the natural world, which means being part of something bigger than themselves, supports the development of these important skills.

Peter: Great busting! Play-Based, you're up! Julie, please bust *building empathy*.

Julie: Empathy is personal. It happens over time as we continually struggle with our place in the world. It cannot and should not ever be on a checklist. As educators, we have the privilege of providing our students with experiences like mirrors and windows that allow them to see both themselves and others. When we invite playful experiences into our classroom, we learn as part of a community.

We experience the world around us through both our own and others' lenses. Daily. With joy.

Peter: Busted! Let's switch it up! Jed, keep busting! Your word is *informal assessment.*

Jed: This one is a piece of cake! Watching students engage in playful learning is hands-down the best way to informally assess students. Are they communicating politely? Are they collaborating to achieve their goals? Are they thinking critically to solve problems? Are their creative juices showcasing their learning in unique ways? All these questions and more can be answered by observing students while they play. Trust me, just watch them and you'll be prouder than a possum on a pancake!

Peter: Well said, Jed! Time to wrap up round two with our final bust. Megan, your word is *inclusion.*

Megan: Our natural world exemplifies the harmony born from a diverse and inclusive ecosystem. All elements of nature—plants, animals, climate—exist in equilibrium, mutually benefiting each other. The flower needs the bee and the bee needs the flower, yet each bee and flower is unique and valuable. Allowing children to see how interconnected nature is—how each individual part plays a vital role in the whole—provides an elegant yet pragmatic springboard for embracing and celebrating inclusion and diversity. Even that pancake-eating possum plays an important part in the ecosystem!

Peter: Beautiful busting everyone! What an even match so far! But I would expect nothing less in the finals of *Which Education Is Best?* It's time to determine a winner in round three—*Best or Bust*! In this final round, after hearing everything your opponent had to say, it's time to tell us why your education is *best* and the other team's education is a *bust.* Team Play-Based, you're up first!

Jed: No way, no how, not gonna do it. These two types of learning go together like butter and biscuits. You can't bust them up! Students need both play *and* nature. This educator just loves a walk "artside." Create, imagine, and play with sticks and stones and flowers and leaves. Just watch the amazingness that happens when you do. You will smile bigger than a rat in rubbish!

Julie: Play is far more than twenty minutes of recess. Each of us has a unique play personality, and we embrace what brings us joy. For students to love learning, educators must welcome play, not just as a behavior but as a mindset. To truly empower our students, we must provide them with experiences they may never have attempted in order to find what might bring them joy, and that might be art, hiking in the woods, crafting a list of jokes or riddles, or every one of those! When we approach education with a playful mindset, we can get fired up by all kinds of experiences.

Interesting perspective, Team Play-Based. I wonder what your thoughts are, Team Nature-Based.

Rachel: I think Jed's spot on, though maybe the butter has melted into his biscuit. What do I mean? For me, nature-based learning *is* play-based—they're inseparable. The only distinction from more mainstream approaches is that in nature-based learning the natural world is a partner in play, contributing objects, space, inspiration, and more. Play-based learning is *great* and play in and with nature is *even better*! All this play and learning with the natural world makes for happy, healthy, curious children. And isn't that the goal of education?

Megan: Clearly, weaving together nature- and play-based philosophies provides the best of both worlds. By allowing children to play in and with their environment, we provide the space for developing kinship with one another and with the natural world while developing critical skills such as curiosity, communication, collaboration, problem solving, resiliency, and a love of learning that can carry them throughout life. The ultimate goal of education should be to develop *life* skills, not grade-level skills.

Peter: What an unexpected and inspiring finish! After seeing these educational models and methodologies battle it out, this well-fought intellectual contest has yielded a winner. Drum roll, please.

And the winner of *Which Education Is Best?* is . . . *both*!

Congratulations, Team Nature-Based and Team Play-Based! It appears that a nature-based and play-based education encompasses the essential elements of an emergent and whole-child approach to learning. But does such an educational experience even exist?

Acknowledgments

To my much better half, Jillian, and our three budding naturalists, thanks for inspiring me to pursue my passion, putting up with my nonstop nature talk, and holding down the family fort while I am working on, writing, and presenting about the trail.

To Amy, Ann, and Courtney, the best kindergarten teammates in the world, thanks for enduring my endless energy, trusting in my vision, and joining me in this natural and playful adventure.

To James Edmond, Linda Hake, and the entire Hamilton School District administration team, thanks for encouraging me to destroy the box and keep pressing forward for the benefit of our school, our district, and our community.

To all my nature-based educator friends, especially Patti and Eliza, thanks for continually pushing me to enhance and enrich the educational experiences of our future leaders.

To all my play people, thanks for inspiring me to pursue and profess the power of play every day.

To Larry, Janet, and the rest of my Retzer family, thanks for collaborating and creating a unique and groundbreaking array of experiences that shine a light on how collaborations can and should be utilized.

To countless community contributors, including Nicole and Dan Jensen of Nic & Dan's Tree Service, the amazing staff of Children's Wisconsin, and the inspirational David Stokes, thanks for all you do to support and sustain nature kindergarten and the entire play-based and nature-infused movement.

To the Woodside Staff, thanks for being risk-takers with me by taking it outside and teaching off trail. You truly make every day a joy.

To the Woodside families and community, thanks for supporting our outdoor initiative and the education of the best students in the world with your time, talents, and treasure.

And last but certainly not least, to my past, present, and future students (my kids!) without whom none of this is possible, thanks for allowing me to be your teacher. Thank you for helping me realize the importance of teaching off trail. And most importantly, thank you for being you!

Introduction

When you hike, the trail won't always be straight and clear. Rocks, roots, and other hazards can trip you up. There are peaks and valleys, some steeper than others. There are curves and switchbacks. And regardless of how well a trail is maintained or what scenery it reveals, the desire to go off trail and explore still calls. Do you stick to the path cleared for you, or do you go off trail and blaze your own journey?

Quite a decision to make.

Going off trail is memorable and meaningful, but it is also controversial. Do the risks of going off trail outweigh the benefits? Are there hazards? Is the area in question ecologically vulnerable? Will your actions leave lasting ecological impacts on the land? When you explore a space outside your own backyard, you must respect the rules of that place. However, in places where it's not prohibited, experiencing nature off trail allows sensory delights that bring outdoor exploration to the next level. Children love picking flowers, treasure trailblazing, and enjoy experimenting with a branch's flexibility. With some common sense and some basic education about respect for the environment, going off trail is an excellent element of responsible outdoor exploration.

When you are teaching, the school year doesn't necessarily follow a straight and clear path. Assessments, meetings, and various responsibilities can interfere with instruction. There are ups and downs, with some years more tumultuous than others, and there are do-overs and setbacks, some more frustrating than others. And regardless of how well you planned or how engaging you think the curriculum is, you will still feel the desire to go off script and try something new. Do you stick verbatim to lesson plans and provided curricular resources, or do you teach off trail and adapt your instruction accordingly?

Again, quite a decision to make.

Similarly, teaching off trail is memorable and meaningful, but it is also controversial. Do the risks of teaching off trail outweigh the benefits? Are there hazards? Are the children in question educationally vulnerable? Will the actions and activities associated with going off trail leave positive and lasting impacts on their learning? When teaching in any school, the expectations of that administration and district should be respected. However, when you can, teaching in a more personalized and passionate manner allows for novel educational experiences that take student learning and professional development to another level. Children love playing games, treasure creative expression, and enjoy experimenting with new and unfamiliar items. With some common sense and basic education about student engagement, motivation, and personalization, teaching off trail is an excellent pathway to effective and efficient child development and education.

This is the decision I made. I wrote this book to share the process, pitfalls, and products of that decision. With play and passion, I teach off trail. I hope after reading this book, you'll do the same.

Education Evolution

Markers and glue sticks are strewn across the floor. A cardboard box has been transformed into a jetpack, paper towel–roll rocket boosters and all. Pieces of felt and clippings from old magazines have been collected and attached to various projects, each serving their own very important purpose. Minutes before, a melodious mixture of celebratory applause and hoots and hollers echoed throughout the room as the Math Championship belt changed hands. A couple of incomplete puzzles and loose pieces cover the counter. A drying rack overflows with coffee-filter turkeys, bingo-dauber trees, and marker-cap pattern trains. A quick scan around the rest of the room shows a swimming pool of stuffed animals, a bookshelf of nature artifacts, a large storage tub of baseball cards, and a menagerie of dress-up clothes and housekeeping items. Anything and

everything you can imagine can be found throughout this classroom—except students.

Where are they?

A quick look out the window, and the mystery is solved. A few
students scale a fallen tree while a few more make adjustments to
their mouse houses. Still others draw in the dirt with sticks. A pair
near the rock pile add bark pieces and dried leaves to their stew.
A couple more are hanging out at their sit spots, observing and
tallying birds in their nature notebooks. A trio of boys turn their
constructed shelter into a pirate ship. Even with their treasure
chest bursting with acorns and seedpods, their hunt for more loot
never ends.

But it wasn't always like this.

On the Wrong Path

Rewind a few years and you would have seen a more traditional
twenty-first-century kindergarten classroom. Bright colors illumi-
nated every wall and chairs neatly surrounded rectangular tables
covered with organized and inventoried color-coded storage
bins. Tablets, laptops, and other state-of-the-art technology were
loaded with the latest reading and math apps, charged and ready
for action. The classroom library was organized by reading levels.
The stoplight pocket chart clearly showed the behavior infractions
observed that day. Everything and everyone had their place. And
they were expected to keep it that way.

Morning equaled literacy, period. A structured reading lesson gave way to specific word work with a big book or poem.
Writing time provided a guided lesson followed by some silent
work time and possibly some sharing time. Phonics drilled and
killed letter sound associations, rhyming, and phonemic awareness. Sight words were introduced, practiced, searched for, practiced again, used in a sight word game or activity, and practiced
again. Eventually they became part of a weekly assessment along
with words utilizing the sound of the week. During stations time,
teacher-selected worksheets and phonics games were assigned
to teacher-selected groups. While those groups worked on their

task, small guided reading or prereading skill groups were pulled for more intense instruction. Anytime during the morning, students who didn't reach a predetermined data point in a certain skill left the room for more direct instruction and practice with a paraprofessional.

After station time, it was time for recess and lunch. Of course, if anyone didn't complete their work, they could just take the first five to ten minutes of their recess (or longer if needed) to finish up. No big deal.

Following recess and lunch, the march back to the classroom led into math time. After a brief look at the calendar, various math topics, including numeral identification, numeral formation, patterns, measurement, number sentences, counting strategies, and addition and subtraction, were taught and practiced using an interactive whiteboard. After completing the lesson, the students broke into predetermined groups to review. Some stayed at the interactive whiteboard for their activity. Others practiced math facts using flash cards. A few other groups used worksheets to dig deeper into the skill of the week or played a math board game. Once the math groups concluded, students gathered around the whiteboard again to copy down numbers and work toward mastery of numeral formation and/or addition and subtraction.

After math, the class traveled to specials, usually two per day: music, art, technology, guidance, or fitness. This period was crucial planning time for the teacher, who utilized every available second to review the literacy and math worksheets collected that day and to copy new ones for the next day. After the class returned from specials and scarfed down a snack, intervention block arrived. If students didn't complete their daily work, needed extra support because they didn't complete it correctly, or lagged in some skill according to collected data, they had some time to finish their work and possibly even work with the teacher.

Then, if time remained, the class might work on science or social studies, but usually in a condensed format. Lots of experiments require setting up and preparing ahead of time, so they were usually skipped, though the teacher might talk about them and see if students could figure out the lesson's objective. If the experiment was completed, rarely did the class discuss the results or troubleshoot anything that happened during the process. There just wasn't time.

At the end of the day each student completed their end-of-the-day jobs, filled out their stoplight charts, reviewed the standards and academic objectives of the day, and maybe even played a little during what was called "choice time." Of course, if work was incomplete, choice time wasn't an option. And if your name wasn't on the green portion of the stoplight chart (clearly visible to everyone at the front of the room), choice time wasn't an option. And if the class needed more time to practice sight words, review math facts, practice lowercase letter formation, preview the next day's lesson, review another skill, or discuss the upcoming assessment, choice time wasn't an option.

But who needed choice time, anyway? It was usually loud, messy, disorganized, and full of bickering and disagreements. On particularly challenging days, the class prepared for dismissal by sitting quietly to think about the mistakes they'd made and brainstorm how they would fix them.

Day after day, week after week, month after month, and year after year, this pattern continued. The students never figured out how to fix it. It took some time, but eventually the teacher did. Well, actually, to be quite honest, he had help.

Rock Bottom

A few more days, and another year of kindergarten would be in the books. What a year of achievement it had been. Amazing assessment data, remarkable running records, and reading levels above and beyond district expectations. Academic success all around. Definitely worth celebrating!

One particular student's success stood out. Having seen her ability and potential, her teacher had individualized much of her work in reading, writing, and math throughout the year, and by the end of the year, all that pushing and prodding paid off. She read at a third-grade level. Her exemplary writing samples included lyrical poetry, thorough nonfiction research, and unbelievably detailed personal narratives. She multiplied independently and displayed extreme articulation in her math reasoning. Of course, her teacher beamed with pride. However, with her drive and enthusiasm for academic success, she would have thrived with or without teacher support. She had scaled an impressive educational mountain with a spectacular view of phenomenal percentiles, delightful data, and superb scores. However, as the end of the school year drew near, she came tumbling down the mountain. And she took the teacher with her.

Anyone who has taught kindergarten in late May and June knows this time of year is a game of survival to avoid bloodshed and maintain sanity. With curricular requirements completed and just a handful of days remaining in the school year, this teacher chose to survive by traveling back in time. Aiming to bring back the sights and sounds of his own kindergarten experience, students played games, sang silly songs, and made art out of anything they could get their hands on—except glitter. Teachers learn many things during teacher training, and although retaining everything is impossible, this teacher distinctly remembered two crucial pieces of advice: first, be nice and friendly to the school secretary, and second, always appreciate the custodian. Nothing severs a positive relationship with custodial staff like glitter. Nothing.

No longer shackled by the monotony of the schedule and the limits of academic-first activities, the kids were just being kids.

These moments unleashed smiles and uncovered skills that had been hidden by the previous tsunami of data and assessments. But the star student's bright shine began to dim, leaving her teacher in the dark.

While her classmates were busy building block cities and feverishly painting in watercolors, the girl watched from afar. When it was time to change shoes for fitness, she tied her laces in mangled knots. During choice time, she refused to share when a peer wanted to use the materials she had chosen. While problem solving with her teacher, she feigned illness when she felt unable to discuss a solution. For nearly 180 days, this superb student had failed to understand or improve the social skills she needed to successfully participate in her classroom community. She lacked problem-solving skills because her studies hadn't required any. She had missed the spirit of kindergarten—the love of learning and the joy of just being oneself. She was a student, not an individual. She was a number, not a learner. Despite her numerous successes, she had been overlooked and forgotten for nearly 180 days, and as a result, she wasn't ready for first grade. She wasn't ready for life. Ultimately, despite incredible academic achievement, she had failed kindergarten. So had her teacher.

I am that teacher.

My short fifteen-minute drive home after school that day felt like forever. I knew my wife and two-month-old daughter were waiting for me at home, ready to snuggle and smile away the stress of another school day. Their presence always quickly erased any-thing that had gone wrong at school—until that day.

Seeing my sweet, innocent child only worsened my condition. As I struggled to understand where my teaching had gone awry, I looked back on my career so far. Though I had taught grades from kindergarten through fourth grade for nearly a decade, earned my master's degree, achieved a national teaching certification in a very rigorous and reflective process, and built wonderful rapport with my colleagues and the students and families I'd had the pleasure to serve, I came to a very painful realization: I would not want my daughter to be in my classroom.

Talk about a gut punch.

I went from beaming with pride to feeling worthless inside. I had hit rock bottom. During the final days of the school year and summer vacation, I contemplated my next move. I briefly considered leaving teaching entirely. But teaching is not just what I do; it is who I am. Quitting was a fleeting idea at best. Still unsure of my next step, I looked at other options within education: Did I need to change grade levels? Did I need a new school? But these only would have bandaged a broken leg. The problem had nothing to do with *where* or *what* I taught; the problem was *how* and *why* I taught. The shimmer of academic successes had blinded me to what truly mattered. I had become distracted from teaching's true purpose by performance pressure and student-learning expectations. My concern for my students revolved around their academics, so if they performed well, I unknowingly looked the other way from anything else they were dealing with in or out of the classroom. Nothing else mattered as long as math scores grew and reading levels soared. I had become everything I dreaded: I didn't teach; I test-prepped. I didn't see children; I saw data points. I didn't prepare them for life; I prepared them for assessments.

I never should have let this happen.

I couldn't let this happen again.

I wouldn't let it.

Not to my students.

Not to my daughter.

Organized Chaos

Before we get too deep into my story, please note that organization is not my strong suit. As my story develops, you'll better understand how disorganization might be better than organization when you're working with five-year-olds. This book may occasionally resemble my classroom: organized chaos. Everyone knows that the shortest distance between two places is a straight line. But where's the fun in that? Like the daily hikes my class takes in our outdoor classroom, we will also go off trail frequently throughout this book, often by design. In fact, I firmly believe it is imperative that students leave the comfort of the trail to blaze their own paths. This may lead to weathering rougher stretches, circling back, and occasionally getting lost, but when students have more control over their own paths, they are more likely to understand and retain the steps taken along the way. You can take the safe route or the adventurous one. Both may lead to the same destination, but will they each provide the same engagement, interaction, and joy along the way?

Think of it like this: At the beginning of each school year, I make two classroom schedules. The first is a cookie-cutter, color-coded, minutes-managed schedule that carefully details when one subject ends and another begins. It is a dream schedule, mainly because it could only happen in my dreams. The second one better mirrors reality. Besides inputting specials, lunch, and recess, it is essentially blank—not because we won't be learning, but because learning can't be scheduled. Each day brings new possibilities, opportunities, and adventures to capitalize on, not schedule or plan.

The key question is, do you control the learning, or does the learning control you?

It took me a while, but I eventually found the answer in my journey as an educator. So come along as I explain my transformational and ongoing journey. Hopefully you'll be inspired to start or continue your own. The *what* will certainly be an integral part of this story, but not nearly as important as the *why*, and hopefully will not overshadow the *how*. Hold on tight for an up-and-down, topsy-turvy ride, with storytelling, practical applications, and humor (or attempts at it), where we'll bend the rules and burst comfort bubbles along the way. We will begin with the redesign of my classroom and the instruction that came with it, then discuss the power and purpose of play. The remainder of the book will showcase how we can and should let nature take the lead. Together we'll explore my educational philosophy, my somewhat unorthodox instructional planning, and the unexpected expectations of doing whatever it takes to help every child succeed.

Fingerpaints and Nap No More

When I tell people I teach kindergarten, they react in a variety of ways. Some laugh, some show surprise, and some ask why, but the reactions essentially fall into two groups: misunderstanding and prejudice. I don't mean to imply that these people are confused or mean, but unless you teach kindergarten today, you can't, and probably won't really understand it. It certainly ain't what it used to be. To make this all a bit clearer and bring you into my world, let me dig deeper into both categories of responses.

1. So Much Fun

The most common response is something like, "Oh, that must be so much fun!" While I can't disagree that working with early learners provides hilarious and unexpected moments, I would not describe teaching kindergarten as *fun*.

When you hear "kindergarten," what comes to mind? Fingerpaints, naptime, play—does any of this ring a bell? Well, in the majority of today's kindergarten classrooms, those things are gone. In recent history, an ever-increasing emphasis on academic achievement has been placed on our youngest learners. I used to joke that I would strike it rich when I designed a standardized test that could be completed in a pregnant woman's second trimester. While that is obviously sarcasm, the truth is that our youngest learners face more pressure to perform than ever before. Simultaneously, for a variety of reasons described later, children come into the educational system less prepared physically, emotionally, and socially to reach these growing (and often developmentally inappropriate) expectations. Society expects more with less. We demand even more from our teachers. Not much fun.

Assessment. There's a dirty word. Teachers cringe when they hear it. I am not here to argue for or against assessment in kindergarten. Truly, I understand both sides of the argument. Assessment helps teachers understand the skills students have and those they have not yet mastered, sometimes termed "lagging skills." Appropriate assessments provide solid information that helps teachers plan instruction. On the other hand, assessment can also create unnecessary stress for both student and teacher. Students have unique learning styles, diverse needs, and different motivations, so assessment may not always be the best way to get to the core of what students can do and decipher what they need. I once saw a quote comparing assessment to popcorn, making a great analogy: "Popcorn is prepared with the same oil at the same temperature and in the same pot. Yet the kernels pop at different times. Don't compare your children to others. Their time to pop will come." When assessment scores guide instructional groupings, plan interventions, and factor into the evaluation of the teacher and the perceived effectiveness of schools, they hold power. Power can be problematic, as can assessing children before they are ready. Not much fun.

Lockdown. The classic and somewhat misleading movie *Kindergarten Cop* had me thinking I would have to ask students to stop climbing tables and chairs. Who would have guessed we now practice hiding underneath them? In a world where violence in schools has become more and more prevalent, schools actively take steps to prepare their staff and students for worst-case scenarios. Think about explaining to an innocent child why this is an important safety drill. Consider sitting in a darkened classroom with more than twenty children for an extended and undetermined length of time. Ponder having development time dedicated to teaching staff when and how to barricade classroom doors and when to flee or fight back against a physical attack. This reality is stressful and sad, and it seems to be getting worse as the country becomes more and more divided. Not much fun.

2. But You're a Guy

Just looking at me, most people would probably not think I taught kindergarten. As I stand over six feet tall and weigh more than two hundred pounds, I might seem out of place in a sea of "littles." Factor in my above-average clumsiness, and one might question whether placing me with children who can easily be squished was the most responsible choice. To some people, seeing a man in an early childhood classroom is like seeing a unicorn. When people find out what I do for a living, more often than I'd like to admit I've been reminded, "But you're a guy."

While I've never considered genitalia to be a determining factor in my ability to work with children, in my experience, overcoming being male is a real thing, especially in early childhood classrooms. That being said, after some initial shock and even confusion, most people I encounter tell me that having more males working with our youngest learners might not be so bad after all. Of course, there are always differences of opinion.

One such difference of opinion caused headaches when I embarked on my kindergarten career. After receiving my initial class list, I also received one of my first (and worst) emails as a kindergarten teacher. Apparently, the fact that I was male did not sit well with one parent. This concerned parent even called the office, asking if "Mr." had been a typo. Paraphrasing, her email described her discomfort in my ability to be the nurturing caretaker required for children at this developmental stage. In her words, I lacked "maternal instincts." This email brought up many feelings for me: confusion, anger, disgust, sadness, and hurt. I felt unwanted and dismissed before I even stepped into the classroom. I also felt extra and unwarranted pressure. I respectfully responded with a request to meet, but it went ignored. All I could do was prove that my ability to teach

was not determined by my physical makeup. (A few years later, this same parent wrote a letter imploring that her other child be placed in my classroom.)

I may not be a traditional-looking kindergarten teacher, but then again, that traditional kindergarten no longer exists.

Radical Redesign

2

While designing my classroom during my early days as a kinder-garten teacher, I displayed bright colors everywhere and stored supplies in neatly organized, color-coded plastic bins and racks. I organized books by guided reading level and placed them in labeled bins, and I strategically covered every possible space in the room with laminated posters of letters, numbers, rules, and inspirational quotes. Each item served a curricular purpose and was safely kept in an appropriate location. I did manage to save room for a dress-up area, housekeeping supplies, a building block area, and some shelves full of random toys and tools. To say my room offered the potential for sensory overload was an understatement.

However, when my students arrived, it became brutally evident that their organizational interests and abilities did not coincide with mine. They didn't use the supplies the way I intended. Their focus strayed from the lessons I tediously planned and prepared. I realized I needed to make changes, and I felt pretty confident about how I would do it. To make room for the ever-growing list of specific curricular resources, I reorganized, ridding myself and my students of many frivolous items. I eliminated the housekeeping toys and dramatically downsized the blocks and building materials. I inventoried the remaining toys and art supplies, then methodically purged those items not associated with my carefully and meticulously prepared curriculum. I lined up the tables and chairs in neat rows, cleared the carpet for morning meetings and lessons, and prominently displayed those educational tools I deemed worthy for student use. I eliminated distractions and, through a wonderful mix of various educational ingredients, devised the perfect recipe for student success to ensure the best teaching and student learning of my career.

Or so I thought.

In the process of designing the "perfect" classroom, I had done much more than just rearrange tables and chairs. I had rearranged my priorities. Worse, I'd unknowingly rearranged the idea of kindergarten for my students and families. Anyone who stepped into my room probably thought they entered a room ready for instruction, assessment, and "learning," but what they really found was a room and a teacher with so much to learn. A teacher who needed a radical redesign.

Hitting rock bottom made it clear that something had to change. My students were succeeding academically at the expense of their social and emotional development. Simply moving furniture around equated to rearranging deck chairs on the *Titanic*. It was clear my goal of creating an academic-centric design had failed my students miserably. So, lest I sank like that immense ship, a redesign was in order: of the room, the curriculum, and most importantly, of myself.

From scheduling to seating, everything I had previously believed and practiced sat on the chopping block. I took a long, hard look at how I structured my classroom, managed my time, and connected with my families. I needed to shake things up, but how? Remembering how my star student could multiply and write paragraphs yet couldn't initiate play or problem solve with her peers, I realized that I needed a tornado of transformation.

The tornado started as a gentle breeze as I made changes little by little. But no matter how much you plan on improving yourself, old habits die hard. What would win out? Intentions? Indecision? Inactivity? Change is difficult, but in my classroom, it was necessary. The first step involved my classroom setup.

My cookie-cutter classroom showcased neatly organized shelves, bright bursts of color, and sensibly arranged tables and chairs. But education shouldn't always be tidy and seamless. Sometimes a jumbled-up puzzle can offer an even better fit. Say goodbye to most of the tables and traditional chairs. Hello bean bags, balance balls, and open floor space. Sayonara bright colors. Hello earth tones. Adios posters. Hello wall space. Plus, welcome back to the building blocks, dress-up materials, housekeeping items, art supplies, board games, and toys, toys, toys. Play returned to the classroom.

Even with the less apparent organization, each decision and element in the redesign was purposeful. Let me explain.

Tables and Chairs

To sit or not to sit? That is the question. I occasionally appreciate the flavor-of-the-day in educational theory, and at the time of my redesign, flexible seating was in fashion. I read articles, talked to my colleagues, and watched online videos of various teachers showcasing their flexible seating arrangements. One thing was clear in my research; flexible seating meant different things to different people. In fact, my own idea of flexible seating today is much different than it was at the onset of my redesign. Initially, I simply interpreted the term literally and thought incorporating fun furniture would solve my problems. I could add new seating options, such as a couch and a few standing desks, and all would be right with the world. Of course, I was wrong. Flexible seating does not mean fun and fancy seats. Much more important is providing students with options and giving them some ownership in deciding where and how they sit. Providing unorthodox items to sit on (or in) can certainly be a part of a flexible-seating classroom, but diversifying the seating situation is far from the only flexibility needed. Teachers need to be flexible in their understanding of what students need physically and emotionally to succeed. Research demonstrates that providing different seating options (or no seats at all) creates certain physical advantages for developing children (Delzer 2016). It also indicates that providing some freedom and flexibility in seating and workspace options helps foster emotional development. Traditional tables and chairs don't always work best for every child. Simply put, *flexible seating* understands this and aims to give children the flexibility they need for a better overall developmental experience.

During my first redesign, I admit I fell for the shiny-object syndrome and used classroom budget money for unique seating options. But this was like taking a baby step in a marathon. Now, while I still provide some more nontraditional seating options (bean bags, rugs, a plastic swimming pool, and kid couches), the real flexibility comes in how the children use them. Can they sit in the swimming pool to write? Is it okay to stand up and use the counter space? How about sprawling out on the carpet? Ultimately, the choice is theirs, until and unless it becomes a problem. The class does have scheduled carpet time, but even then students have options if their bodies need them. Do students (and the teacher) need time to figure out these needs? Yes. Do these needs change over time? Definitely. Can offering unique chair options and more freedom in the classroom lead to issues that might be curtailed with traditional teacher-assigned seating? Of course. As with just about everything we expect from children, it takes teaching, time, practice, and more practice to get things moving in the right direction. It takes even more time and practice to keep it going that way.

Overall, when you really get down to the core of the issue, it is all about control. In my opinion, when children feel they have some control, they tend to feel happier and perform better, both academically and developmentally, showing better emotional regulation and better cooperation and collaboration. And maybe, just maybe, giving up some of that control can help teachers teach better as well.

Colors and Space

The annual beginning-of-the-year Tetris game of fitting everything into the classroom could be easily avoided with one slight shift. Rather than create a space for my students, I needed to create the space *with* them. While I did have a general layout of tables, tools, and toys, I left open spaces and blank walls. Open space, a luxury in prior configurations, became more of a focal point in the redesign. This saved tons of time during the frantic beginning of the year as I focused less on what the room looked like and paid more attention to the students who really make the room what it is. This also gave students more ownership over their classroom's design.

In fact, space was an essential element of the redesign. I wanted to make sure the classroom had room to grow and evolve as the year progressed. Rather than create a room designed around my instruction, my goal for the room was to showcase the children according to their interests and their needs, across all developmental areas. But without having met the students, I did not know their interests, motivations, or learning styles. I trusted that as they arrived with their own flair and personalities, the classroom would change accordingly. As children grow and change over the school year, so, sensibly, should their classroom.

Normally I organize the walls to prepare for the meet-and-greet event that introduces students and families to their classroom, plastering them with colored construction-paper bulletin boards and various curricular-content posters to showcase what we will learn in the year ahead. However, in the redesign, I instead took a minimalist approach by putting up fewer items, knowing that student interest would (and should) drive what to place there and when. Eventually student work, student art, and student-led learning outcomes and activities would fill those empty wall spaces.

Many teachers take immense pride in their classroom's design and organization, viewing their classrooms as a direct reflection of their teaching. When I redesigned my room, I knew some might find it unusual or consider me unprepared, but I was willing to take that risk. I felt my previous classroom design highlighting academics had masked my inability to prepare students for anything other than assessments. Not only did my new design lack glitz and glam, but the open spaces around the room and on the walls gave the classroom a sort of deserted, unfinished feel. But I had to look past how my room might be perceived and focus on what it would soon become. Word of warning: students designing the room can lead to clashing colors, off-centered bulletin boards, and potential sensory overload. That might drive type A personalities a little crazy, but it matches our classroom personality just fine.

Toys and Tools

Ever heard the expression "Go big or go home"? Well, when I decided to bring back the toys and tools I previously found unnecessary and distracting, I went big. Besides bringing back items from earlier years, I sought and secured many more. My overall classroom concept revolved around increasing the open space by removing tables and chairs. Less-than-traditional items intended to encourage play and exploration filled up some of this newly opened space: a swimming pool filled with stuffed animals, sports equipment like a miniature basketball hoop and hockey goals, and a four-person tent. Later I added a whole new area that would epitomize our classroom: a nature center. We'll get back to that later.

I rescued housekeeping items from storage in the school's basement and revived the dress-up area, refreshing it with clothing and accessories purchased from rummage sales and second-hand stores, which are wonderful places to find random board games, puzzles, toys, and trinkets. I especially enjoy picking up gizmos, gadgets, and whatchamacallits. When students pick up an item and aren't sure what it is or what it does, creativity is born. This is why I also added a loose-parts library to my radical redesign. Initially paired with an expanded art cart and creativity corner, I added dried-out marker tops, discarded toilet-paper rolls, bottle caps, and other "useless junk." I also kept my local dollar store in business with frequent trips to keep the art cart fully stocked with googly eyes, popsicle sticks, pom-poms, and foam

stickers. Both the time and mostly non-reimbursed funds spent on these shopping excursions are worth it when you see student excitement and engagement in action. Give students a bag of old buttons, some discarded PVC pipe, and a bingo dauber, and then just sit back and watch innovation and creativity take over.

Anyone who has seen my classroom knows that I haven't yet found a "perfect" design. Every year (and often even more than once in the same year), I move things around, take things out, and add things. Maybe I need to keep things fresh or maybe I get bored quickly, but either way, my classroom is definitely flexible. It's always interesting when older students come back to visit and mention how different the room looks. Sometimes I wonder if I should just pick a design and stick with it. But then I really think about my classroom and why the setup changes every year. The answer is quite simple. Because I change. And more importantly, because the children do too.

Finding a classroom design that merely utilizes space is easy, but finding one that works is a different story. I am blessed to have a large room with an adjacent storage closet, so I am able to rotate materials in and out as needed, whether to enhance the curriculum or connect to student interest. As the year progresses, I add decorations, resources, toys, and art supplies for intrigue and interest. I want my students to consider our classroom their second home and feel both physically and emotionally comfortable here. For eight hours a day and nine months of the year, school is their home, so they might as well enjoy it. Maybe they'll even become true partners in their educational experience. I want and need my students to feel free to be who they truly are so their personalities can shine. My classroom design is not mine at all—it is ours.

The Power and Possibility of Play

3

Changes in my classroom's atmosphere seemed inevitable, considering its new open-space concept, the new materials, and the return of old favorites. Would the students be louder? Probably. Would the room be messier? Most likely. Would I make changes to the schedule to allow time for more creative exploration and unstructured play? Without question. Did those possibilities lead me to second-guess my radical redesign? Not for a second. My educational decisions should not be based on how others might perceive my room and what happens in it, but on what is best for my students.

Producing Production?

In my radical redesign, perception didn't matter—production did. When educators prioritize students' developmental needs as the driving force behind their educational decisions, student production improves.

Student production. What does that even mean? Assessment scores? Reaching or exceeding curricular standards? Overall academic achievement? These definitions seem eerily similar to the issues that inspired my radical redesign in the first place. Hmmm.

Luckily, my definition of student production extends well beyond academics. It includes, but is not limited to, skills such as critical thinking, problem solving, communication, creativity, fine and gross motor skills, emotional regulation, empathy, focus, resiliency, executive function, collaboration, and risk-taking. Encompassing important skills across the developmental spectrum might seem overwhelming, and in all honesty, it often feels that way too. But it doesn't have to. There is a simple solution that was lost while educators, administrators, and districts competed for the latest and greatest methods of improving student production. This overlooked tool can instantly improve every facet of student production. It's not assessment. It's not mindfulness. It's not fitness. It's all of those and so much more wrapped up in one simple and easy-to-use package. To improve student production, play. That's it—play. All students need is the time, space, and opportunity to play (Dearybury and Jones 2020).

So why, in many cases, is play being taken away? There is a myriad of reasons, but many of them revolve around increasing academic expectations for our youngest learners. In a groundbreaking book, *Crisis in the Kindergarten*, researchers showed that "children now spend far more time being taught and tested on literacy and math skills than they do learning through play and exploration, exercising their bodies, and using their imaginations" (Miller and Almon 2009, 11). Essentially, schools have shifted away from play, exploration, and social interactions as they move toward prescriptive curricula, test preparation, and building academic skills. This shift increases expectations for all parties in the educational process, from individual students to whole districts. And if these expectations aren't met, the blame is laid on students or teachers, not on the expectations themselves.

As these expectations rise for our earliest learners, academic interventions increase as well. More and more, children are removed from their classrooms to work on academic skills when assessments show their work isn't up to par with these rising expectations. However, research suggests that young children learn more when their learning is play-based and self-directed rather than teacher-led (Fisher et al. 2013). Despite this, children are pressured to achieve academic success at younger and younger ages. In my experience, students who don't meet rising expectations are often recommended for extra support at younger ages, regardless of the developmental appropriateness of such intervention. While many teachers find this illogical, inefficient, or downright cruel, they go along with it due to the competitive pressure (real or imagined) of their own expectations, the expectations of their school or district, and the growing need to prove their worth to society at large.

In many cases, the academic progress made by their students determines a sizable portion of an educator's evaluation—and subsequent salary. This practice, known as performance or merit pay, aims to financially reward teachers according to the academic progress of their students. However, the pros and cons of this practice are highly debatable—while merit pay has been shown to improve test scores, it has produced little to no effect on student outcomes such as retention and application of knowledge (Pham, Nguyen, and Springer 2020). Simply put, teaching to the test improves test scores, not learning. On top of this, teachers are often required to explain and describe any and all steps they take in furthering the academic progress of their students, even those they find developmentally inappropriate. This phenomenon, known as "pushdown academics," particularly as tied to performance on standardized tests, leads to depersonalized educational environments as both teachers and students feel reduced to mere pieces of data (Hutchings 2015; Bradbury and Roberts-Holmes 2016). This increased emphasis on high-stakes testing also has significantly decreased the amount of time and space dedicated to play.

Administrators, even entire school districts, face similar pressures to meet these growth and improvement benchmarks and are assessed and measured according to these same expectations. Local and state governments often tie their school and district funding to academic success. When the controversial No Child Left Behind legislation was introduced in 2001, it stated that schools that fail to meet its Adequate Yearly Progress standards, which measure a school's academic growth, may not be permitted to access certain grants and other forms of funding. While this legislation has been replaced, new laws, including the Every Student Succeeds Act, still emphasize annual testing, rigorous standards, accountability, and state and local school report cards. School districts seek high marks on these report cards, but it comes potentially at the expense of what might be better for students.

Many in the field of early childhood education feel that educational decisions have become less and less tied to educational experience and expertise. The pressure to perform and "achieve" sadly supersedes child development, best instructional practices, and developmentally appropriate methodology. For instance, even though research has shown time and time again that play is vital to a child's development, it is slowly being eroded from our educational system and is in some cases on the verge of extinction. This is especially evident in socioeconomically disadvantaged schools and districts. In a 2015 interview for the National Association for the Education of Young Children, early childhood consultant Ijumaa Jordan sums up this inequity by warning that where more assessments and regulations are administered, the unintentional consequence has been to decrease play and increase teacher-directed activities to teach skills that are intended to close the achievement gaps reported in assessments (Jordan 2016). These educational reforms restrict access to self-initiated, complex play for low-income children, children of color, and American Indian children.

The hard work districts, schools, and teachers have done to develop processes and programs to help children succeed across the developmental spectrum has proven one simple concept: students can reach these rising expectations. However, this also stirs up a much more complex question: should they have to?

The Kindergarten Paradox

The answer might lie in something I call the kindergarten paradox. This paradox relates to the growing gap between the increased expectations placed on children as they enter school and the fact that so many of these children enter the educational system with a diminished set of skills necessary for school success. Basically, we ask our children to do more with less. Sound familiar? Maybe because it is also what many public schools are being forced to do in an era of budget crunching and protecting bottom lines. I am not a politician by any means, but I have a basic understanding of budgets and am aware that funds should be used as appropriately and efficiently as possible. Schools and teachers have been asked to do more with less, time and time again, and are always up for the challenge.

Students also show a great deal of resiliency and adaptability. But continuing to take away opportunities for children to develop skills while simultaneously demanding they do more is not only unrealistic, it's wrong. Society has engaged in lengthy discussions about why children enter school with lagging skills, but are these skills even developmentally appropriate? In my opinion, many of these so-called "essential" skills, including mastering letter sounds, independently constructing sentences, and proficiently demonstrating various mathematical strategies, are not essential at all, at least not at the age children are expected to achieve them. In other words, I firmly believe that instead of placing greater and greater academic expectations on younger and younger students, early childhood education needs to systemically change its focus to cultivating and supporting developmentally appropriate social and emotional skills. These foundational learning skills can be developed in a kind of "if you build it, they will come" manner. (Apologies if you've never seen *Field of Dreams*.) Meaning, if the schools servicing our youngest learners de-emphasize academics and instead build environments designed to foster creativity, expression, problem solving, critical thinking, and every other element that defines play, the academic skills will come. More importantly, they will stay.

I had the honor of speaking at an educational forum that high-lighted the kindergarten paradox. In this forum, educators, parents, and community members convened to discuss early childhood education in today's society. Many topics came to light, including student and educator anxiety, stress, and time management. The forum also featured a healthy discussion on the importance of family and community support and the struggles endured when that support is lacking. It was evident that many people feel confused and frustrated about current educational expectations. We explored why these expectations continually rise with no end in sight, and more importantly discussed what we could do to change this and why change is necessary.

Similar to the goal of increasing student production, eliminating this paradox is essential to the happiness and health of our youngest learners. Is reaching these goals possible? Yes, and they can both be achieved through one simple solution.

Play.

The Purpose of Play

One of the joys of play is that it means different things to different people. Whatever your definition, researchers agree that play is positive for children and adults. Play has significant benefits in many areas of development, including academics. A 2019 paper, "Taking Back Kindergarten," details how "play serves a critical role in the development of long-term cognitive skills that will enable children to become college and career ready" (Silverman 2019, 16). Research demonstrates that children who experience more active, child-initiated early learning experiences perform better in later school years. Early educators have long been creating this type of learning environment and doing so effectively. Kindergarten should be leading the way, not following the trade winds of education policy.

Yet, despite all the positive outcomes play produces for children, it seems to be disappearing. In the home setting, play has changed dramatically due to a variety of societal factors. In the academic setting, it is not uncommon for play to be viewed as a waste of time and subsequently pushed aside. Play is often considered a break from work or a reward for students who complete their jobs, and when used this way, skipping it or removing it entirely from the daily schedule becomes more acceptable. Even teachers who appreciate play can be caught limiting it when crunched for time. For some children, play is disappearing. For others, it is simply evolving. Either way, it is worth investigating some potential explanations to better understand reasons for diminishing or disappearing play at both home and school.

It is important to note that these explanations are generalizations. Just as each family's home life differs, no explanation can be a one-size-fits-all box. However, I feel these explanations for the loss of play at home are applicable across a variety of settings and family dynamics. I categorize these reasons into four separate but often intertwined groups: technology, overscheduling, parental perception, and the banishment of boredom.

Technology has done a great deal for society. It adds convenience, enhances communication, and is generally understood to be a necessity for living in today's world. It also has gigantic impacts on play. It provides outlets for creative and critical thinking and creates avenues for individuals to connect and play with others from all around the world. Technology-based play allows for unique and evolving play opportunities, such as virtual field trips and online gaming. However, technology also has pitfalls. An overreliance on technology can interfere with problem solving, and an attachment to technology can cause children to miss out on developing important motor skills, which potentially leads to physical problems. Additionally, many people worry about the effect technology has on personal communication and basic social behavior. While technology-based play provides opportunities for creative and critical thinking, this type of play doesn't embody the full body and spirit of true play.

Though technology can make life easier, it can also make overscheduling and overprogramming children's time too easy. Enrolling children in multiple structured activities takes away from the spontaneity of unstructured play, formerly a staple of childhood. Sizable chunks of time for quality play are difficult to find when children are shuffled from school to soccer to swimming to tae kwon do to anything and everything else. By filling their schedules and taking away their ability to make their own play, we instill in them an overreliance on others, which sets children up for failure. Maybe we overschedule children because we overschedule ourselves as adults, with or without children. We have many chores and errands to run, and our own lists seem to be never-ending. Adding the responsibility of raising children to the mix makes time management even trickier, especially when we have unin-

tentionally conditioned children to rely on adults or screens for their entertainment. Overscheduling causes overscheduling. It's a vicious cycle that impedes the power of play.

In an idyllic view of the "good ol' days," children played outside and didn't come home until the streetlights went on. Climbing trees. Catching critters. Living life. And doing it without an adult in sight. Those days are now few and far between for most of today's generation. In today's world, unstructured, unsupervised play is nearly extinct. In fact, researchers find that a myriad of factors are at the root of this decline: parental restriction, physical and neighborhood environments, societal beliefs about parental roles, and a diminished sense of community (Clark et al. 2015). But while societal and parental views about play and children have changed, have the children themselves changed? Would today's children thrive if given earlier generations' freedom and opportunity to enjoy play? Though research suggests they would, we will likely never find out because current trends don't give children that chance. For a number of families, the world is too dangerous. For many others, it is perceived to be. What about kidnappers and neighborhood violence? What about litigation if a child gets hurt in someone's yard? But most importantly, what would the neighbors think or do? To some, allowing children to play and explore so independently exemplifies careless, lazy, or apathetic parenting. Adults must be in control all the time, setting the schedule, making the rules, and creating play opportunities for their children. It's their responsibility. Between potential dangers and the power of parental perceptions, play is certainly different today.

When did being bored at home become unacceptable? Children are rarely afforded the unplugged and unsupervised free time they need to decompress and inspire creativity. A need for constant entertainment and action thwarts true play. The banishment of boredom has negatively affected children's ability to think creatively, use their imaginations, and show resilience when things go awry. Many parents can attest to the frustration their child shows when they feel they have "nothing to do." Is this because children have too many distractions that don't allow time for free play? Is it because they don't have enough experience even to know where to start? Regardless of the reasons, whether it be an overreliance on technology, a lack of time, a potentially negative parental perception, or the inability to handle boredom, children today have plenty of obstacles to overcome to enjoy play in their home life.

In school the problems with play are similar. First off, technology has become more and more prevalent in schools. Technology can certainly simplify certain classroom tasks. Whether it is in data collection, family communication, or the globalization of education, technology is transforming how student work and information is collected, analyzed, and used to make decisions. However, just like technology at home, there are drawbacks like overreliance and distractibility. Children are plugged in more than ever before. Consider the virtual learning necessitated by the COVID-19 pandemic. Students of all ages and abilities were forced into some type of screen-based schooling. Teaching kindergarten already felt like herding cats, and the distractions and difficulties of navigating an online classroom exacerbated that situation. Building the trust and confidence required to empower early learners is a formidable task when the main transmission of information lacks the personalization of a face-to-face setting.

Overscheduling is also a school issue. Time in the classroom is often micromanaged by curricular and assessment requirements. With pressure from seemingly every direction, play is a luxury, and teachers avoid giving up instructional time to allow for play. Even though many teachers know that play benefits children, there's just no room for it on an already overflowing plate of planning, instruction, assessment, intervention, and documentation.

But that isn't the only reason teachers might push play to the back burner. While parents may fear litigation and being considered lazy or inattentive by letting their children play freely, teachers don't want to be labeled "that teacher" or have the noisy or disorganized room. Play can be loud. Play can be messy. Play can be misunderstood. Teachers may avoid misunderstandings by simply minimizing the time, space, and opportunity for students to engage in free play.

Boredom exists at school. But banishing boredom has become a school's responsibility. Besides teaching to the rising expectations, teachers also need to capture and keep the attention of entertainment-starved children accustomed to multiple options to tamp down their boredom. Ask any teacher and I am sure they can relate to being told by family members that (eyes rolling) boredom is the root of a student's behavior issues, and if we want to avoid behavior issues, we just need to teach better. In reality, we just need to let children play.

Play is going away. The paradox is real. Student production is expected to increase at all costs and often with fewer resources. Yet rather than eliminating play or ignoring the benefits of it for children, play should be embraced and increased for everyone, adults included. Until play is valued for what it is and what it does, for the betterment of all, I fear the trend of disappearing play at home and in school will only continue.

So, what exactly is play, and why is it so important? I'm glad you asked.

What Is Play?

Play is quite frankly impossible to define. While many have tried to come up with a simple, all-encompassing definition for play, these attempts are always too simplistic and lack specifics. Play is a multifaceted creative expression often associated with recreation and entertainment. While it is mostly linked to children, play is for everyone. That said, play for you might be completely different than play for me. Any one definition is unlikely to fit everyone's personal play characteristics. However, regardless of differences in play personalities, there are some consistencies among them.

- Play is fun and desirable to engage in time and time again. Anyone in the midst of play is usually happy and content.

- Play is incessantly sought after. People play voluntarily because it stimulates the mind and body. People desire to maintain their state of play for as long as possible.

- Play can be a social equalizer. When engaged in play, differences that are often highlighted in non-play settings can be diminished.

- Play is purposeless. There usually isn't an end goal when it comes to play. It is a release from the pressures and structure of everyday life.

- Play offers the potential for improvisation. Rules are flexible. The rigidity of the world is erased as play evolves and changes instantaneously.

- Play is better when it is authentic. If it is forced, it loses value and its positive outcomes are minimized.

Regardless of how it is defined or described, play offers amazing possibilities for growth across the developmental spectrum. It is the epitome of whole-child development. Play positively affects physical development. Active play is associated with improvements in fine and gross motor skills, endurance, balance, and coordination. Even rough-and-tumble play, often banned in schools, offers important benefits, such as improved body control and spatial awareness. Play also strengthens immune systems and cardiovascular health while improving flexibility and agility. Increased mental health, including better stress management and lower levels of depression and anxiety, is also linked to consistent time involved in play.

Play fortifies the mind and enhances cognition. When playing, individuals apply critical thinking, risk-taking, and resiliency. They grow in independent thinking. Simultaneously, play provides them valuable opportunities for creative expression and imagination. Academic skills, such as language development, mathematical reasoning and logic, inquiry, and various literacy skills are also practiced during play. On top of that, play promotes a love of learning.

Play strengthens social skills by being deeply rooted in cooperation, collaboration, and negotiation, and it emphasizes inclusion. Sharing, empathy, and understanding different points of view are also intrinsic to play. When there are social issues, conflict resolution, compassion, and attention are all imperative to the problem-solving process. These skills are also crucial to play. Play boosts emotional regulation. Play builds self-esteem, confidence, and impulse control while at the same time increasing levels of happiness in those involved. Play helps develop coping skills and adaptability. Play heals. Play is joy.

We all need more play. Many researchers have spent countless hours proving it. More writers have produced numerous articles explaining it. Even more teachers and parents have spent endless hours advocating for it. Yet, despite volumes and volumes of supporting research and invaluable experience, if we all just sat and observed children, we would figure out what they already know and show naturally. Play is good. Real play, that is, not inauthentic, forced play. Watching children deep in play is an amazing and inspiring sight. However, something happens as children grow up. Many adults lose their way, and play becomes a chore or a waste of time. It is not considered serious—though for children, play is of the utmost importance. It is their work. It is their socialization. It is their learning. It is their right. It is not only what they want but what they need.

And bringing it back into my classroom and curriculum was exactly what I needed as well.

Make the Minutes Matter

Every August, teachers deep in the trenches of classroom preparation await the arrival of a crucial email from their administrator. This email holds the holy grail of beginning-of-the-year planning: the schedule. This schedule informs teachers what time their lunch is, which days might be best to sign up for recess duty, and what time each day their precious prep time falls. More importantly, the arrival of this information sets off the rat race to "make the minutes." Teachers make the minutes each year when they lay out the details of their daily schedule, making sure to include all the curricular minutes required by the district and state. Now, this process is merely a figment of the imagination, as it can't possibly represent an actual day's events. Many daily occurrences aren't counted but are quite important to young learners. In fact, if you ever ask a kindergartener about their school day, there is a good chance that one of these uncounted, unimportant events is what they will most want to discuss. Bathroom breaks seem innocent, but they often aren't. It takes plenty of time to teach, practice, and reach the expectations for these breaks. Snacktime is also a major event, especially if the snack is something the child enjoys. Handing out and enjoying birthday treats is one of a student's most anticipated moments. For various reasons, hallway travel takes much longer than one might expect. If students see friends, neighbors, or siblings along the way, it's essentially impossible to keep their focus on the task of getting from point A to point B. It's also commonplace to have multiple stops for students to tie their shoes. And no matter how many times you try to avoid it, students get lost or displaced from their class.

(By the way, they get lost throughout the year, not just the first few days.) Many daily minutes disappear during classroom transitions. Plus, if you teach in a winter climate, you know the pain of putting gear on, taking it off, and repeating the process over and over and over again. And brain breaks are necessary for everyone's sanity, teachers included. "Making the minutes" is an arduous process. Some even consider it a ridiculous hoop teachers and schools must jump through to appease the licensing and regulation gods at the state and national levels. But despite this, we accept the reality that every minute in school is crucial.

Overall, society has incredible, and rising, expectations of what children should be able to do and when, and as they rise, more time is needed to reach them (or try to). Unfortunately, these expectations don't necessarily mesh with either research-based best practices or plain old common sense. School is now businesslike and results-based. In many cases, school closely resembles a factory, churning out student after student on a conveyor belt lined with assessment data and standardized test scores. The pressures students and teachers feel from these assessments can and—often does—stunt their creativity and ability to succeed. These added responsibilities create cookie-cutter classrooms and curriculums as teachers are left with less time to individualize their teaching.

There is never enough time to meet the myriad expectations in education, but we cannot allow this to discourage us. Complaining about what is out of our control may be cathartic, but words can only do so much. Teachers may not be able to directly change the expectations placed on themselves and their students, but they can look at how they interact with their students and families. This is where they can be the change by making change. *Asking* teachers to change what they do or how they do it is daunting, but *forcing* them to change destroys morale. The key is to show them why change is necessary, how it can be done effectively, and how implementing it positively affects things they care about, like time management, student achievement, classroom community, whole-child development, and the overall health and happiness of both students and teachers.

My radical redesign emphasizes that it doesn't matter if you make the minutes if the minutes you make don't matter.

Sometimes you make slight adjustments to your hairstyle. Sometimes you buzz your head and start over. My radical redesign was a total depilation. In addition to redesigning my classroom, I revamped my classroom schedule. Knowing that children had been missing out on vital unstructured play, I infused play opportunities directly into my schedule. While an outsider might wonder why I decided to use up valuable instructional minutes on play, I felt confident that providing those opportunities would yield important benefits. Besides supporting lagging skills, play is an ultimate classroom community builder. I decided to start each day with play. I wanted my students to be able to freely choose their first interactions of their day. I wanted them to have some control over their choices and feel that school is not just their workplace, but a place where they can enjoy themselves and the company of their peers. Traditionally, a teacher prepares a worksheet for children to complete each morning, which provides them with both academic development and time-management practice. Harmless, right? But is it actually helpful? That's debatable. For some students, it is a breeze, but for others, not so much. For the latter, morning work sets the tone with stress, avoidance, and frustration before the day really even starts. Rather than beginning the day under teacher control, I let the children be the decision makers. Adding play to the start of the day is a simple and effective way to change.

Of course, having play to end the day wouldn't hurt either. Why not schedule play in the middle of the day? Better yet, why schedule play at all? Increase your flexibility and your common sense and take play breaks as needed. Trust me, you'll know. Even better yet, insert play opportunities directly into the standards and objectives of the curriculum. When students struggle with inattentiveness, burst with extra doses of energy, or need a pick-me-up after a tedious task, play offers the perfect ingredients for cooking up a healthy classroom atmosphere. Musical play, kinesthetic play, creative play, free play—no matter how you do it, just play. I have found that incorporating more play into the day offers students opportunities to release energy, exhibit creativity, and become more comfortable in their classroom community. In fact, the more I add play, the more I want to add even *more* play.

That said, scheduling play isn't synonymous with structuring play. For play to produce the benefits I have mentioned, it must be child-directed. Telling children how to play, when to play, and where to play hinders their play and actually creates play problems. Giving up control can be tricky, but it is worth it. We don't need to teach children to play, as it is a natural process for children. However, certain elements of play benefit from our reinforcement. Connecting play to social-emotional instruction can enhance play's productivity. Whether the lesson is initiating play, problem solving, or active listening, connecting play with the bodies and hearts of children improves relationships in the classroom community.

While I engage in play as much as possible at the beginning of the school year, I spend most of that time observing. Besides getting to learn about the play personalities of my students, I also scan my room, taking note of what works well and what needs tweaking. My students and I make adjustments together through class discussions, role-playing, and instruction. These observations and their teachable moments are vital to the success of my play-based classroom. While I aim to inspire student-led play that encourages whole-child development, I also am well aware that students come into the classroom with varied play experiences and that my ultimate job is to keep them socially, emotionally, and physically safe. By guiding them to create a positive play environment for everyone, I am preparing them for a year of success both in and out of the classroom.

Because success means much more than academic achievement, play and academics are not mutually exclusive. Remember, for children, play is work. Serious work. However, as teachers, we are responsible for teaching learning standards and reaching curricular expectations. That responsibility often intimidates teachers and prevents them from integrating play into their schedule and instruction. However, I feel adamant that these responsibilities must include play as much as possible. We know play is fun and that it positively influences every area of development.

Unfortunately, we forget how play benefits cognitive development. As mentioned earlier, play improves cognition. Knowing this, including play as a resource in your instructional toolbox is an effective and efficient strategy for promoting a happy and healthy classroom. The amount of play resources available online is incredible—morning meeting activities, technological apps, and games across every subject area mean a classroom could potentially play all day every day without skipping an academic beat, if not jump a few steps ahead. Then throw in opportunities to play outside, and reap all the whole-child benefits of outdoor exploration. What a wonderful classroom that would be!

Fun Is Not Extinct

Maybe it's my love of donuts and Dr Pepper, but my energy level is through the roof most of the time. I try to channel my excess energy into something fun because, let's face it, teaching isn't always fun. Creating an environment where students learn and work while having fun is a skill all teachers either have or should have. Fun brings learning to life. Fun should not be extinct in education.

Play and fun follow me wherever I go. It's hard for me to stay serious for extended periods of time. Even the various part-time jobs I've held while being a teacher exemplify fun and playfulness. While they supplement my income, they mainly fulfill my need for fun. Ever given tours of a world-class zoo while driving a Zoomobile that resembles three extended golf carts linked together? I have, and years later, I still remember the speech. Ever stuff yourself into an oversized sausage costume to run a legit race around the warning track of a major league ballpark? Guilty as charged. In fact, I have won races as all five sausages, though I do have my favorites. I could write a few other books on this topic alone. One for children and one for adults.

Fun doesn't have to stop once you enter the classroom door. In fact, the fun starts *on* my classroom door, with a decorated sign labeled Classroom Zoo. For years this has been my theme. I don't mean my students are wild and stinky (though that's debatable some days). I consider a zoo to be a place where the diversity of every animal is celebrated. I want my students to have the courage and confidence to be who they are instead of trying to be like everyone else. Who wants to see a zoo full of the same animals in every exhibit? Not me. I like variety, which is why every day in our classroom is unpredictable. I have a schedule, but it's not set in stone. I have lesson plans and curriculum maps, but they're as flexible as rubber bands and bounce like playground balls. But if you couldn't see our room, you'd most likely hear it. I'm loud and proud, especially when it comes to having fun. We sing. We dance. We laugh. We build. We create. We play. While our activities change rapidly, one thing stays constant. We are noisy. Learning is messy and loud. Who wants to walk into a room of perpetual silence and staleness? Not me—I like action. I'm sure the sights and sounds of the classroom zoo drive more organized, traditional teachers and staff in my building nuts, but it's who I am, and if you can't be yourself, who are you?

Playfulness is engaging, memorable, and above all, fun. Here are some more simple ways to insert fun back into your classroom while still connecting to curricular standards.

Play music. Often. One day you'll hear Beethoven; the next day, polka. Heck, I'll play just about anything except country. Sorry, I have my standards. Expose children to the diversity music offers. We have class songs: Shakira's *Try Everything* is catchy and promotes the wonderful and needed lesson that mistakes are okay, and Sara Bareilles's *Brave* showcases the importance of being true to yourself. Per class tradition, we pack up the last few minutes of the week rocking out with toy microphones, strumming replica guitars, and air drumming to Europe's 1980s rock anthem *The Final Countdown*. Want to have more fun with poetry? Practice a poem until it is memorized, then try reciting it to different musical genres. Trust me, it's a blast belting out *A Chubby Little Snowman* as a folk singer, opera singer, or hip-hop superstar. Investigate websites that focus on enjoying and creating music, like *Go Noodle* and *Incredibox*. My class is also known for chanting. We have nature chants, play chants, math chants, reading chants, loud chants, quiet chants, silent chants, birthday chants, and animal chants, just to name a few. If you can chant about it, we probably do.

Co-construct silly stories. To review story elements, we create a silly story together. My students brainstorm the characters, setting, and problem for a story, and then I combine these class-created elements with a solution of my own. The new silly story is born when I write the story down and the children illustrate the pages. These become extremely popular picks from our classroom library.

Dust off the costumes and introduce characters. Detective Dargatz shows up most often during our morning meeting activities, though he has been known to help find mystery words in phonics or share clues during scientific investigations. Foreman Dargatz's specialty is reminding students of the writing tools they need, though he has also been known to help construct stories and fortify broken relationships. Chef Dargatz cooks up ingredients for number stories, though his menu also offers word chunks, rhyming words, and his famous alphabet soup and syllable stew.

Let the students dress up as well. Have costumes and props available. Allow children to showcase their hidden personalities by providing them time, space, and opportunities to use their imaginations. Make sure one such object is a replica wrestling championship belt. Not only does it inspire interesting student reactions, but it can be a tool for learning. In my classroom, the championship belt changes hands regularly though a counting game called Math Championship.

Bring back board games. Board games cultivate many academic and social skills, so we intentionally devote instructional time to them. Once students feel comfortable, the games become available during choice time. Eventually they are added into learning stations and become an activity children do at home too.

Introduce loose parts. What do toilet paper rolls, bottle caps, empty milk jugs, and cardboard boxes have in common? Not much at first glance, but to a curious and creative child, they can become building blocks for a castle, ingredients for a cake, or materials for a racetrack. Loose parts are random objects most people might otherwise discard. However, they provide a great outlet for imaginary play and saving interesting junk for this purpose is a great alternative to throwing things away.

Set aside time for art. Students need time to explore materials and bring their imaginations to life. Keeping an art area stocked, introducing different supplies, and providing time to explore these materials gives students a healthy way to inspire each other to try new ideas. Share art with your students by taking them on virtual field trips to online museums and art galleries. Art is everywhere.

Connect with local and regional authors. To liven up our reading instruction, I designed a Wisconsin Picture Book Pen Pal program. Every month or so, we dig deep into a picture book by a Wisconsin author, then use the book as inspiration for art projects, skits, and writing activities. We also write a class letter to the author, asking questions about the book, being a writer, and anything else a kindergarten mind can come up with. Because I connect with the authors beforehand to get them on board, they respond to our letters with letters of their own. At the end of our time together, we host the author for an in-person or virtual visit.

Host regular theme days. To break the monotony of week in and week out, pep up the class in a long stretch of school with no holidays, or connect to something that is happening in the world, host a special day based on a particular theme. For example, as colder weather approaches, we celebrate our study of animals preparing for winter with a Hibernation Day by building dens, eating plenty of snacks, and cozying up to a stack of books in our pajamas and sleeping bags. A few days every school year, we hold Play Days, which is exactly what it sounds like—we literally play all day in various ways. Our Surprise Snow Day is always the most memorable, probably because it is impromptu. Every winter, when the class hits a lull and needs rejuvenation, we spend a day falling in love with winter by building snowmen, snowshoeing, and making fun winter-themed snacks. When spring arrives, we celebrate America's favorite pastime with a Baseball Day. We make personalized pennants, create our own baseball cards, devour a tailgate lunch, and of course, run a sausage race in honor of our hometown team, the Milwaukee Brewers.

Children are fun. Playing is fun. Teaching can and should be fun. Have fun with it!

The Power of Perception

Meeting parents for the first time at the beginning of every school year is an exciting and exhausting event. Whether through a beginning-of-the-year letter, an open house event, or a more formal face-to-face meeting, both teachers and parents seek to make the best possible first impressions. Positive relationships between home and school provide benefits for all parties, especially the student. As a male in an early childhood classroom, I try (probably too hard) to set the best possible tone. I often feel I have more to prove since I am a man. Because my personal experience has showed that some people have a harder time accepting males as caregivers, I previously overcompensated by using humor and silliness to win over parents. I also have an annoying habit of talking louder than I need to most of the time. The teacher three doors down from me mentions she can hear my Weedwacker of a voice more than she probably wants to. When talking, I am easily distracted. I also tend to talk in circles, repeating things again and again. I also tend to talk in circles, repeating things again and again. I also tend to . . . See what I mean? Did I mention I also sing? All the time and usually off-key. I actually won a national choral award in high school, but I don't know what happened since then.

Luckily, I am naturally playful, and my classroom families quickly see that. In fact, word of my playful personality spread quickly. It was brought to my attention that parents of incoming kindergarteners had been told that if their child was placed in my room, they would "play all day." Initially, I felt embarrassed when I heard this. I didn't think that interpretation was true or becoming. I felt it made me seem immature, like I didn't take my professional responsibilities seriously. Sure, we played—and I am definitely silly. But we all worked hard, including me. I began to doubt my abilities and lose trust in how I utilized play in my classroom. The power of perception influenced how I felt about my playful room. I worried that parents would get the wrong impression of me.

What I'm About

Early in the school year, I host voluntary family information nights to help my students' parents better understand my classroom environment and philosophy, give them a sense of who I am as a person and teacher, and lay out an overview of the kindergarten year. I present information on a variety of topics, including my play-based educational philosophy, my methods for communicating with families, my homework (or lack thereof) policy, and the general logistics of kindergarten and school. I always begin each session by pulling at their heartstrings, telling them the story of my star student who changed everything for me. I follow this emotional appeal by digging deep into the unique elements of my play-based classroom. A few of these topics are detailed below.

Stop the Stoplight

Despite the occasional feeling adults have that "kids should know how to behave," most don't—so instruction is necessary. Children are *not* inherently naughty, but the gap between what schools and classrooms see as acceptable behavior and what children need as developmentally appropriate practice is often wider than what teachers and parents expect. These expectations can be taught in a number of ways, though modeling and practice are crucial. Explaining this during these information nights is a first step in introducing parents and families to a whole-child approach to early childhood development, as opposed to simply improving or managing child behavior.

Besides obvious interest in their child's academic development, parents also want to know how their child behaves in school. Educators use various methods to document and track these behaviors, such as moving labeled clothespins or using the good ol' fashioned stoplight system. These methods and others often include some sort of visual aid where all can see the current "behavior" of a particular student, which brings the potential of public shaming and embarrassment. It also leads to what I call meaningless motivation. This means students might show initial motivation to "stay on green" or "not have their clothespin moved," but that motivation does not translate into actually changing the behaviors and actions that are detrimental to a safe and healthy learning environment. Seen by adults as acknowledging student behavior, but often felt by students as punishing, these visual representations of behavior management end up acting as methods of student control. As I often tell my students, "you can't control what others say and do, but you can control how you respond to it." I believe schools shouldn't focus on controlling student behavior, but instead aim for appropriate and child-edifying responses to it.

I am not too proud to admit that I used a stoplight chart for a long time. I even made a tech-friendly version I could throw on the interactive whiteboard and a fancy sheet the kids colored every day as part of their end-of-the-day responsibilities. When students strayed from green, we had a chat at the end of the day, but I noticed a pattern: similar chats, similar students, over and over, yet behaviors didn't change. Our pep talks weren't working. I wasn't helping children find success in the classroom, I was training them how to be sneaky and dishonest. Rather than concentrating on making better choices, they focused on not getting caught making "naughty" ones. To the students, the stoplight chart equaled punishment, not progress.

Similarly, communication between students and families suffered. Discussions often veered from the students themselves to a laser focus on the chart. If greens were consistent, life was good. But if a red came home, watch out. Students did anything and everything to avoid moving off green, including lying, bartering, changing colors, or constantly losing or forgetting their stoplight sheets so they didn't make it home. It was a mess, and I needed to find a way to clean it up.

So I tossed the stoplight chart and changed the three colors to faces: a smiling face, a neutral face, and an uneasy one. I also connected these faces to our school expectations to give it more of a global and consistent perspective across school settings. Unfortunately, as you may have already predicted, my faces sheet essentially became the new version of the stoplight. When it came time to fill out their sheets, it was much easier for students to manipulate a facial expression than to change a stoplight color. Though well-intentioned, my new method for communicating student behavior to parents had only introduced new behaviors like coercion, avoidance, and dishonesty.

Knowing my faces weren't working but still wanting a way to consistently communicate students' social and behavioral progress with their families, I took a U-turn. For years my communication about behavior emphasized what students did or didn't do. Actions and inaction took precedent. I was ignoring an essential part of social-emotional development: I failed to recognize feelings. Children often didn't know why they were on yellow or asked to draw an uneasy face. Simply put, they didn't connect their behaviors to the symbols on the sheet. When I realized this, I tweaked my communication sheet. It still had various faces. It still had a space for my comments. It still included a spot for a family response. The tweak came in the verbiage. The sheet no longer aimed to document what a student *did*—it focused on how a student *felt*. We took time to connect certain faces to different feelings, and if an issue came up at recess, we discussed it as a class. If we saw problems during playtime, we problem solved together and made connections to various feelings. We still took time each afternoon to fill out our sheet. It wasn't perfect. Some students seemed happy all day but drew a teary face because they skinned their knee at recess. Some constantly struggled with listening and following directions but felt perfectly fine and drew a big smile. Yet asking children to draw their own faces allowed them daily opportunities to express their feelings in a less coercive and controlled way. I also had the flexibility to document and share pertinent behavioral information, both positive and in need of improvement, with the family. Each day, I selected a few students and added quick notes on an accomplishment, a funny occurrence, or an encouragement. While I noted any social and behavior issues that had popped up, I focused on sharing little tidbits that could spark conversation at home. Changing this communication sheet flipped around the way I looked at behavior. Trying to control behaviors is impractical and irresponsible. Building relationships with students and families alike is a much better method for improving and sustaining positive student behavior.

Taking time to dissect a situation and connect it to feelings was trickier and more time-consuming than slapping on a red-yellow-green label, but it was meaningful for the teacher, for the family, and most importantly, for the student. Schools are seeing a need for more social and emotional instruction, and we are understanding how it positively correlates with student behavior and school community. That being said, the process is flawed if a school increases social-emotional instructional methodologies for the sole purpose of controlling behavior in hopes of increasing academic output or performance. The social and emotional welfare of the child should supersede any particular academic objective. Focusing on this aspect of child development is more effective than the traditional stoplight method or a sheet full of faces, whether the teacher uses social-emotional curriculum, methods of mindfulness, or more focused and intentional instruction around schoolwide expectations.

Play Profiles

But this is school, and while social and emotional development is important, academics rightfully play a major role in what parents want to know about their child's educational experience. One of my biggest obstacles when working with parents is proving why play and relationship building pave the way for that sought-after academic improvement. I feel one of the best ways to get to know the children and help them get to know each other is through child-led play. In the beginning of the year, I offer multiple opportunities for play every day. Usually these play opportunities are preceded by a simple lesson on a newly introduced object or a reminder about classroom expectations. After each session, we discuss how the play went by noting observations from myself and students. During play, I join in when possible, though most of my time involves observing students in their play and documenting what I see.

In my observation work, I use a tool I have created called a *play profile*. This two-sided sheet documents play observations and serves as a useful tool to prove that play is not only important for the students' social and emotional development but also for achieving academic standards. The first side contains logistical information, including the date, what the student played, who the student played with, and the area of the classroom where the student played. Over time this information helps me identify trends and play patterns. I use this information for making student groupings, planning instruction, and communicating with families. The second side includes various descriptors from the district report card organized by subject area and research-based, developmentally appropriate early childhood standards not covered by the report card.

www.peterdargatz.com/
teaching-off-trail

www.peterdargatz.com/
teaching-off-trail

During play opportunities throughout the day, I focus on a handful of students, obtaining at least one observation for each child every week. In the first quarter of the school year, I focus on the front side, documenting the who, what, and where of the child's play. I share this information at the fall parent-teacher conferences, as these initial conferences focus more on each child's social development and adjustment to kindergarten than academics. As the year progresses, more emphasis and time are placed on the back side, connecting play to the specific report card descriptors and early childhood standards. This validates my play-based approach by providing specific examples of how students can and do reach academic expectations in play.

Homeplay

To me, *homework* is a dirty word and should never be used in kindergarten (or most grades, in my opinion). However, students of all ages and abilities commonly leave school with a backpack full of work meant to help them learn. While I could write a dissertation on my distaste for homework, I won't bore you. I'll give you a very abridged version.

Homework doesn't improve school readiness, attitudes toward education, or achievement. I could share dozens and dozens of scholarly and research articles proving homework is unreliable and unnecessary, but early childhood education expert Alfie Kohn sums this up perfectly in his book *The Homework Myth* (2006). "Homework," he writes, "is a reliable extinguisher of curiosity" (p. 17).

However, knowing that many in my profession don't feel as strongly as I do about this topic, I knew I had to find middle ground to appease my families and give my students some experience with the tortures—I mean "homework opportunities"—awaiting them in their future schooling. I call this middle ground *homeplay*.

Homeplay is similar to homework in that it is done at home. That's about the only similarity. Homeplay is meant to be legitimate skill practice, not meaningless memorization or draining busywork. The skills involved go well beyond academics, though children might learn a few educational tricks along the way. Homeplay is also optional. I assigned these opportunities for practicing skills at home hoping they would become more of a routine because they were fun and unique, not because students and parents were under pressure to please the teacher or felt anxious about consequences associated with incomplete work.

Homeplay is essentially just what it sounds like—play. Some general examples of homeplay are:

- Call a grandparent and tell them about your school day.

- Go stargazing.

- Play a new board game.

- Find a book at the library about your favorite animal or place.

- Ask a parent to teach you a new chore.

- Take a walk outside and count the number of birds you see.

- Challenge someone to a game of Rock, Paper, Scissors.

- Play Nature BINGO, suggesting curricular-connected nature activities families can enjoy together each month.

www.peterdargatz.com/
teaching-off-trail

But Will She Read?

Hosting family information sessions lets me give parents information about my philosophy, which hopefully eases any concerns and clears up any misconceptions they may have about our classroom. I want families to walk out understanding that this is *our* classroom. With that in mind, I reinforce the need for a positive relationship between school and home, as such a partnership is a huge asset in a child's education. Additionally, considering the elements detailed above, especially my homeplay and parent communication methodologies, family participation outside the classroom walls is not only appreciated but essential. I want to make that point crystal clear while also allowing for family input. So, after giving my presentation, I always open the floor for questions.

Everything I had already discussed was nearly jeopardized with one of these questions.

The parent started off saying some very positive things. Knowing the art of the compliment sandwich, I waited for the other shoe to drop. She said their daughter loved the first few weeks and came home excited to share her experiences. She mentioned how comfortable her child felt in the school and our budding classroom community. But then, in just a split second, her happy tone abruptly changed when she asked: "I appreciate you making your classroom so fun and inviting for my daughter, but will she read?"

I shrugged off her concern with a generic and weak response that I don't even recall now, but later I came to realize just how important that question is and why I needed to become very intentional in my response to this concern. If I wanted to be taken seriously and show that my less-traditional style is purposeful, I needed to be more proactive in communicating my philosophy in a way that explains my rationale while also allowing for parents' input. I knew that while only one parent had mustered enough courage to ask that simple question, others likely shared it. While I felt most parents understood and even approved of my approach, I also sensed they might have been a bit worried about the results of this play-based classroom compared to a more academic-first approach. I believed the changes I had already made and those I would eventually make would empower my students, and in turn, my instructional techniques and philosophy would create a better classroom community for my students and families. And that's more than an opinion.

To satisfactorily demonstrate why I did the things I did and, more importantly, why my approach is good for students across all academic areas, I realized I had to hit the books. I read professional articles, publications, and books on play. I searched for ways to improve the whole-child development of my students without interfering with the instructional responsibilities of my public school setting. In both formal and informal settings, I had conversations with teachers, administrators, and parents to verbalize and get feedback on my internal struggles and goals associated with my changing philosophy. Through all my research, reading, and real-life experiences, what I found was encouraging.

More and more research dedicated to early childhood education continually demonstrates that the overemphasis on academics for our youngest learners is due to the "pushdown academics" mentioned earlier. Experts in child development and early childhood education agree that pressuring children and educators to reach increased academic expectations does not improve student performance and learning, especially if that pressure coincides with the removal of play. In an eye-opening research article detailing the effects of play-based learning on early childhood education and development, researchers concluded that "the benefits of play-based learning outweigh the traditional methods of teaching. . . . Students are encouraged to continue fostering their understanding of independence, build social skills, social-emotional development, motor function, and so forth. It is incomprehensible to assume a child will have mastered these skills within the time span of one academic year. For this reason, it is necessary to continue this play-based mode of learning throughout the entirety of one's early childhood experiences (from birth to eight years old)" (Akhtar et al. 2018).

It is important to think of the process of learning as a marathon, not a sprint. I've never seen a child get on a two-wheeler for the first time and ride off independently. It's a process. Training wheels on. Short successes. Training wheels off. More short successes with assistance. Then, eventually, those successes become independent. Similarly, new learning is often teacher led, accompanied by plenty of support. That support slowly fades away, and eventually the student is asked to complete tasks on their own. In that process, students must make mistakes. Even at the kindergarten level, many children equate intelligence with correct answers. They can be "blinded by the right," only recognizing correct answers as progress. They seem to feel that mistakes must be avoided or hidden. Children seem to believe that errors either mean you weren't listening to directions or you just aren't smart enough. You'd be amazed at how much time in class is spent focused on battling this belief. Of course, it is true that some mistakes happen due to off-task behaviors or a lack of listening. They're kids. That comes with the territory. Regardless, something in our educational system and society needs to change. Failures must be allowed and even celebrated. Failures are the offspring of risk and effort. Take off the training wheels and get on the bike, even at the risk of falling.

When that parent asked me if her daughter would read, I felt she was really asking a bigger question: *What will my daughter learn?* In her book *Lisa Murphy on Play: The Foundation of Children's Learning*, the early childhood specialist answers this question perfectly when she states that "within the foundation of children's learning, play is the cement that holds the foundation together. Playful learning is how children get ready for school" (p. 165). Essentially, if you want your child to learn the best way they can, have them play.

It seemed clear to me that more play was just what my classroom needed, and based on my research, the experts agreed. But would my families? I needed a way to communicate this to them. Like the old adage says, *actions speak louder than words*.

Transforming my classroom required a shift in family communication. I now build deeper and more thoughtful relationships with families by using a combination of my aforementioned communication sheet, a phone call schedule that includes more frequent check-ins, and offering more homeplay and interactive opportunities. Knowing some families may feel confused about or disagree with my homework (or the lack thereof) philosophy, I strive to share my rationale for it with them. Though research-based evidence and educational articles certainly support my philosophical shift, I sought to create opportunities for sharing our playful learning in more meaningful and memorable ways. Not in a newsletter, not in an email—but in action. Families don't need me to explain play-based philosophy when they can see it in action or, better yet, be a part of it. My open-door policy allows parents to join us anytime they are available. In my experience, a simple invitation into the classroom eases anxiety parents might have about the ins and outs of the classroom, even if that parent has no intention of taking up that invitation. For families who are unable to visit, the aforementioned homeplay opportunities extend learning at home in a method that worksheets and computer apps could never replicate.

When I changed my classroom and philosophy, I reinvented my communication style. I still talk loud. I still talk too fast. I still get sidetracked and struggle to stay on topic. But now my focus has shifted. I thrive on building rapport with my students. I often give students silly nicknames. I joke that I use their nicknames so much, if they come back and visit years later, I'll remember their nicknames instead of their actual names. I recognize that communication is much more than just talking. I talk less. I listen more. But I listen to much more than their words. By paying attention to their nonverbal cues and clues, I am better preparing them to achieve success and gain confidence across the developmental spectrum. By watching them in play, I am giving them the opportunity to develop in ways that better suit their interests and learning styles. Play gives children the power to express themselves in ways that transcend their still-developing communication skills. Figuring out effective ways to communicate with children is imperative. Anyone who has ever had a conversation with a five-year-old knows that topics switch at the drop of a hat, information gets repeated ad nauseum, and the point of the discussion often gets lost in translation. However, flip the script and think about how teachers may seem just as meandering, repetitive, and confusing to a child.

Every part of my radical redesign, from updating my communication methods to inserting more play, served a pivotal role in the next steps of my education evolution. Every step moves the process forward, even if you take a misstep along the way. Not every path taken leads you in the right direction. But wandering doesn't necessarily mean you are lost, and some risks are worth taking.

Take It Outside

My most vivid childhood memories revolve around creative and imaginative unstructured play. I am the youngest of four kids and the only boy, so a good deal of this play was solo. I remember blasting professional wrestling entrance music, strutting down the hall, and entering my living room as if it were a wrestling ring. I acted out matches with my Ultimate Warrior wrestling doll, always making a dramatic comeback to snatch victory from the brink of defeat. I remember playing tennis against myself on the side of my brick house—I never lost. I also played basketball with my backyard hoop, pretending to nail buzzer-beaters time after time. Inside, I played billiards in my basement with an uneven and slightly wobbly pool table. To this day, playing on a level table is always a disaster because I still factor in the curves caused by the unevenness of that table. I regularly battled my father in Wiffle Ball, keeping stats along the way. My cousins and I created various games that often became heated events. Ever play hand hockey in a basement full of antiques? We did. Ever play basketball with one player armed with a large fishing net to block the shot? We did. Ever play street football at dusk, dodging parked cars and fire hydrants? We did.

Of course, risky play is also a cherished childhood memory. With my proclivity for using table tennis paddles to fling billiard balls all over the place, it is an absolute miracle I never needed any emergency dental work. We held countless pillow fights in the dark, somehow avoiding serious injury. And when we filled plastic handheld squirt guns with gasoline and sprayed a lighter to make a flamethrower, it's amazing we didn't burn down the garage or each other. While some of our energy found outlets in activities that were hazardous and downright ridiculous, the spirit of creativity and the desire to engage in excitement and risk were consistently at the core of our play.

This creativity extended into our play in nature. I was fortunate to have had some semiwild spaces in my neighborhood. The creek at the end of my street has since been restored to a more natural setting, but in my youth it was edged in concrete, with a few man-made waterfalls highlighting the otherwise straight flow of the water. We used these waterfalls as the start and finish lines for our stick races. We also caught frogs and lured crayfish out of the muck with raw bacon on the ends of sticks. Another memory involves buckets of worms. On one particular rainy afternoon when the worms had evacuated their saturated underground homes and cluttered the curb line, I devised a plan to save them from what I felt sure was certain doom. I filled up a few of my sandbox buckets with water and rescued quite a collection of wiggly, watery worms. Of course, I unintentionally sent them all to death by drowning. Or so I thought. Turns out earthworms don't drown, and their untimely demise was more likely connected to the level of oxygen in the water I used to collect them. The beauty about learning in nature is that even when you think you know it all, there's so much left to learn.

While this story lacks a happy ending, it does show my burgeoning interest in the natural world. Maybe my buckets of worms were a sign that my affinity for and inquisitiveness about nature would continue into my adult life. I may not be accidentally killing buckets full of worms anymore, but an experience a few years back filled my personal bucket with nature-based interest and intrigue. On a random country drive, my wife and I noticed a small congregation of cars parked on the side of the road. As we were in the middle of a very rural community without any noticeable landmarks nearby, we wondered why these cars were there. Upon closer inspection, we saw a sign indicating that we had unexpectedly come upon a trailhead for the Ice Age National Scenic Trail. Neither of us were very familiar with the trail, though it reminded me of a snippet from the social studies textbook I used as a fourth-grade teacher. We grabbed a flyer at the trail sign, and before we knew it, we had joined our local chapter of the Ice Age Trail Alliance and become volunteers for the trail, participating in trail improvement days and spreading awareness of the trail whenever possible.

I took my volunteer work further when I created a Tyke Hike program aimed at getting young children and families out on the trail. My wife and I had just had our first child. We saw the benefits of being outside and wanted to provide as many opportunities as possible for our growing family. As I led more and more hikes, I noticed other families felt the same way. Then it hit me: I loved taking children out on the Ice Age Trail, I loved being in nature and learning from it, I loved teaching, and I did all these things in my volunteer work. Could I do them in my career? I had already added more play into my classroom. Was it possible to add even more outside of it?

The Article (and the Two Women) That Changed It All— Again

Nature and *school*. *Play* and *nature*. *Kindergarten* and *outside*. My random online search using word combinations like these pulled up a plethora of new information. Article after article backing my budding beliefs about play and time in nature filled my computer screen. But one article caught my eye more than any other. And that one article changed everything—again.

Patti Bailie is the article's author. She was also the founding director of the Schlitz Audubon Nature Preschool in my favorite city in the world: Milwaukee, Wisconsin. This innovative and influential nature-based preschool works side by side with a fantastic nature center on the shores of Lake Michigan, and happens to be just fifteen minutes from my home. I had heard of the Schlitz Audubon Nature Center before, but only because I had attended a family wedding there. I knew absolutely nothing about its nature-based preschool program, and I had never heard of Patti Bailie. The first thing that grabbed my attention was the article's title: "Forest School in Public School: Is It Possible?" Amazingly, this was essentially the question I'd been asking myself in my research. After reading the article multiple times, I felt like it had been written for me. One of the most intriguing concepts the article described was something called forest kindergarten. Further research showed me that this outdoor educational approach is common in Europe and has been slowly creeping into the American educational system. This article inspired me to do more research, which quickly snowballed as I became overwhelmed and confused about the different terms I encountered. *Nature preschool. Forest kindergarten. Forest school. Nature kindergarten.* With a little more digging, I began to parse out the similarities and differences between these concepts. These terms aren't quite synonymous, but they all work toward getting students outside. And that was what mattered to me.

Even though Patti Bailie no longer worked for the Audubon, I felt compelled to reach out to her. In a weird way, sending the email felt like calling a crush in high school. Would I sound desperate? Was there even a chance I could take this idea to the next level, or would it crash and burn? Would she even respond? Luckily for me, she did.

We exchanged a few emails before deciding to communicate over the phone. I distinctly remember calling one weekday afternoon during her university office hours, near the start of summer vacation. While my wife and daughter played inside, I headed to our concrete slab of a patio out back, notebook in hand. Though she shared a wealth of information about potential resources and roadblocks, she seemed more interested in learning about me and asking questions about my ideas. I appreciated her interest. Our conversation whetted my appetite for learning even more. I tried my best to jot everything down in my chicken-scratch scribble, hoping to leave the conversation with at least a sapling from the massive forest of wisdom she generously imparted.

Patti provided tons of helpful resources worth investigating. However, her greatest gift might have been a name: Eliza Minnucci. Just like me, Eliza is a kindergarten teacher in a public school. Just like me, Eliza had felt that something needed to change. Just like me, Eliza had felt the best way to make that change was to take the classroom outside. However, one significant difference existed between Eliza and me. Her hopes and dreams for taking students outside were not just hopes and dreams like mine—they were her reality.

Eliza is one of the creators of a program known as Forest Fridays. As the name implies, students spent Mondays through Thursdays in their regular indoor classroom. The class transformed on Fridays with trips to the nearby woods. For the entire day, the class immersed themselves in nature, engaging in various activities that support whole-child development: working with tools, cooking snacks, observing wildlife, journaling, building shelters, and exploring the forest. You name it, they did it. And it worked! The program made headlines, and schools in other areas began replicating it. Forest Fridays continues to set an excellent example of nature-based education for schools around the world. Patti mentioned Eliza and recommended that I reach out to her to ask whether she could provide any insight or inspiration for my situation. We spoke, and after receiving personalized advice and ideas from Eliza about my simple research, I knew that taking my classroom outside was not just the direction I wanted; it was the one I needed.

But could that need be fulfilled in *my* public school? Before this outdoor idea engulfed me, the thought of leaving my school had never crossed my mind, but now that I knew I needed to be able to take students outside, I came to realize that if I couldn't go outside at my current school, I couldn't stay there. Now that I'd learned of successful public school outdoor learning programs, I felt compelled to start the process of creating my own. After continuing the conversations with Patti, she suggested that I visit nearby nature-based programs. Since she was the former director of the Schlitz Audubon Nature Preschool, I figured that would be the right place to start. I connected with its director and visited. If love at first sight is a real thing, this might have been it. I loved everything about it—the students, the land, the staff. After the observation, I sat down with the director. Without really even noticing it, the casual conversation unexpectedly morphed into an interview. As I sat there answering questions about my current employment situation and my budding beliefs about nature-based early childhood education, I came to realize a few things. First, preschool teachers are saints and deserve so much more recognition and compensation. Second, while I was flattered that the nature preschool thought so highly of me and felt that I would fit in seamlessly with their staff, I then knew in my heart that my mission was to bring nature-based opportunities to the school and staff I already knew and loved.

Now that I had a better grasp on all the things I wanted to accomplish, I had to figure out how to communicate these aspirations to my district's decision makers. This step was as crucial as anything else I had already done. These decision makers could easily ground the idea before it even took flight. Do I lead with the heart or with the head? Should I share my personal passions or rely on research-based evidence? Would it be better to toe the line and stay with the status quo or go off trail and potentially disrupt the waters? Only one way to find out.

Twists and Turns

In the waning weeks of the school year, classrooms across the country are in survival mode as summer-itis (totally real) sets in for students and teachers and the school year trudges to an end. Though the school days are still the same length in actual hours and minutes, something about that time of year makes time crawl. If a snail, a sloth, a tortoise, and a June school day raced, I don't know who would win, but I'd put my money on the June school day finishing a distant fourth.

Teachers wrap up their curricular responsibilities and hold on to every last bit of patience and sanity left in the fibers of their depleted beings. They prepare for a much-needed break to recharge and rejuvenate their minds and bodies. After months of rigorous work, students prepare for the summer that is just beyond their grasp. They're ready for a well-deserved vacation from traditional learning and tight schedules. While teachers and students anticipate the end of another year at school, families set summer schedules and gear up for their children being back at home. Every member of the education system experiences an odd mix of exhaustion and excitement.

But the end of this year felt different to me. My excitement far exceeded my exhaustion. While my first year organizing a play-based classroom had been successful, my work had only just begun. I had done extensive research into outdoor education and formed a bare-bones idea for implementing it. I stared at the physical manifestation of my idea every time I looked out the window. Behind my school was an unused parcel of retired grazing land, scattered with mature oak trees and blanketed in goldenrod. The space was unappreciated and unutilized as a scenic backdrop to the school. It needed to *be* our school. I was ready to share my ideas with the world and get this outdoor educational adventure started. The first step was emailing my principal and associate principal.

The second I hit Send, one of the longest and most emotional roller coaster rides of my life slowly started creeping up that first hill of the track. In my initial email, I generically requested a meeting to discuss an idea. Keep in mind, it was early June, and everyone was suffering from an overdose of meetings. Fortunately, both of my direct administrators agreed to meet. I met with them and candidly communicated my need to continue to transform my classroom and instruction. I included information about outdoor kindergartens and similar programs I had researched, using a degree of salesmanship to detail how a program like this would set our school apart. Both administrators displayed confidence in my thought process and seemed inspired by my passionate plea for change. Of course, confidence and inspiration can only go so far. Action was needed. But before I could get moving, they informed me that I would need to connect with district administration. With their blessing, they also suggested I chat with the rest of the kindergarten team. I left the meeting pleased that my idea hadn't been squashed. I followed up with a thank-you email to both principals. Of course, I also attached the article from Patti Bailie and a link to Eliza's Forest Fridays website. I could take a breath. After this initial ascent and descent, I could see the next twists and turns coming up. First, talk to my team.

My team, the fearsome foursome. Through thick and thin, they are there. They are more than a group of teachers, more than a group of friends—they are family. When I moved from fourth grade to kindergarten, I quickly realized that this was where I was meant to be. Not just because of the children I would be blessed to teach, but because of the team I joined. From day one, we clicked. As always, families have disagreements and don't see eye to eye on everything, but in the end, love wins out. We are four completely different individuals with unique styles, strengths, and talents, yet, put us together, and we are one. We know when to be serious and when to have fun. We *get* each other, and we *get* kindergarten.

If you look up *kindergarten teacher* in the dictionary, you ought to see a picture of Amy "Hugabug" Hilgenberg. We share the same birthday and wedding anniversary. Since she is the eldest of our group, we joke with her that when she retires, we're all going with her. Next up is Ann Tamblingson. Not only is she on my team, but she lives across the street from me, so she's lucky (or cursed) also to see me on weekends. I'm proud my children call her Auntie Ann. Last but not least is Courtney Klein, my adopted little sister. I grew up the baby of my family with three older sisters, so Courtney takes the brunt of my big-brother aspirations. Her room is right next to mine, so she gets to see (and hear) me often. I couldn't imagine working with any other team.

To prepare the team for my plans, I sent them an email requesting an afterschool conversation. However, with all our students out of the classroom and at specials at that moment, the team came over right away. I guess my odd request for an impromptu meeting so close to the end of their year piqued their interest. After assuring them everything was okay, I shared my idea. I wanted them to understand my passion, but I also didn't want anything forced on them. However, we were all aware of how things tend to work in schools. If my plan was successful, as I knew it could be, the team would inevitably feel "positive pressure" from parents or administration to join in. I wanted to keep them informed, encourage their feedback, and most importantly, receive their blessing. Being responsible educators, they had questions and wanted to dig deeper into my intentions and goals. I sent them resources and kept them updated on my progress. With their approval, I felt comfortable pressing forward. So far I had navigated the loops and swoops of this roller coaster without much backlash, but the ride was far from over. Next up, district administration.

I emailed the director of curriculum, sharing the gist of my idea along with a request to meet. Within a few days, I was sitting in her office along with our director of human resources—two of the district's most influential decision makers. When we met, my nervous excitement produced fumbled words and jumbled thoughts. As I had in my meetings with my principals and kindergarten team, I shared my research and connected it to some of the district's goals and initiatives. Based on the amount and type of questions they asked me, the concept seemed well received, and I felt cautiously optimistic about moving forward. The three of us all left the meeting with homework. The director of curriculum would present the idea to the superintendent. The director of human resources would investigate the idea with the facilities and grounds manager. I was tasked with creating a document of important information regarding my ideas. The reasoning. The rationale. How it would fit in the goals and mission of the district. How it would be implemented. Logistics. Potential obstacles. Basically, a dissertation on my entire outdoor vision. With summer break on the horizon, we planned to talk again soon.

Now that I had disseminated my thoughts out loud to the powers that be, I needed to get them down on paper in a coherent manner. Anyone who knows me knows clarity isn't necessarily my greatest asset, but taking risks is the name of the game, so I got started. Being a bit cheesy and knowing that sometimes catchy names go a long way, I titled my plan Growing Inside by Going Outside: An Outdoor Vision for the Hamilton School District. I made sure to include a favorite photo from one of my Ice Age Trail Tyke Hikes on the cover. It featured a young boy sitting in the grass, looking at a nearby marsh. The composition and lighting of the photograph made it look almost as if he was looking into the future.

I felt very motivated to get my vision written, but after a long and arduous school year, starting summer break glued to a computer screen was tough. Still, I forged forward. Typing a mile a minute, using my best hunting-and-pecking strategies, I tried to formulate a comprehensive document that would win over my district. Besides taking occasional play breaks with my daughter and dogs, I typed. During one of these typing sessions, I received an email that left me with a twinge in my stomach. It was from the director of curriculum. After meeting with some district officials, she wanted to talk. Was this the end of the ride? Was the district politely but swiftly responding with a thanks-but-no-thanks? I wouldn't know until I called. When I did, I was relieved to find out that she had been talking to other district staff members about my ideas, and based on those conversations, she identified some additional steps I needed to take before a decision could be made. She asked me to meet again later in July to "discuss a few things further," requesting that I bring my vision with me.

After a fast and furious few weeks, July arrived. Writing halted while I led my first Saunters summer school class for the Ice Age Trail Alliance. This outdoor course teaches children about the Ice Age National Scenic Trail by hiking it for a week. After a successful session leading kids out on the trail, I felt better than ever about taking my classroom outside. Now I just had to finish writing about it. Lacking the experience of a professional proposal producer, I wasn't sure how much information was too much. I wrote about the benefits of going outside. I connected those benefits to the mission of the district. I wrote tentative plans for my "outside day" and included lessons and their curricular connections. I wrapped up with some specific resources and examples of other programs I had researched throughout the process. Before turning in my proposal to the district, I sent it to Patti and Eliza, and their helpful feedback pointed me in a better direction. In my vision, I had called my outdoor day *Wednesdays in the Woods*. Catchy, huh? However, Eliza advised against singling it out or giving it a cutesy name. Rather, I should acknowledge it as just another part of my methodology. Even though it is inherently different, I should treat it like a normal part of my class, not anything unique or extraordinary. Then, once the program gained traction, it could become whatever I wanted it to be.

After more editing and revising, I sent it off to my district contacts. Maybe it was nerves or the sweltering mid-July heat, but waiting for the "discuss a few things further" conversation caused me considerable anxious anticipation. I have never played the waiting game well. When the calendar turned to August, I finally got the call to meet. Several district staff members had walked the unused land behind the school I intended to use for our outdoor learning space. This walk had conjured up more questions than answers. During our face-to-face meeting, district representatives respectfully barraged me with those questions. The meeting

focused on important but less-than-thrilling topics. Obstacles. Accountability. Specific curriculum. Parent communication. Safety. The district showed interest but wanted to have a strong game plan on the front end to ease possible parental concern and opposition. While this made sense to me, I felt somewhat overwhelmed and under-prepared to problem solve on the spot. Luckily for me, I didn't have to. Instead, I got more homework! I was to ponder everything discussed and get back to the district as soon as I could. I wasn't too worried though. I had two pretty impressive teachers. I emailed Patti and Eliza again for their insight, and, feeling optimistic, I soon reported back to the district. But the up-and-down roller coaster of emotions was about to take another turn.

While I connected with my experts, the district had found an expert of their own. Our director of curriculum had met Larry Kascht, a nature center director, while attending an education conference. After sharing my plans with him about transforming the grounds behind the school to implement an outdoor kindergarten, she invited him to come check out the land and give his thoughts about its possibilities and pitfalls. She contacted me to set up a time when we could all get together. Someone else had joined the ride.

In preparation for the meeting, I received permission to mow a path through the land to give it more of a realistic feel. Before I fired up my tiny red mower, I called a few friends for help. I had been volunteering with my local chapter of the Ice Age Trail Alliance for over a year now and had met several amazingly generous and experienced trail builders. I wanted to see if they had any insights about the land that could help move my plans forward. I emailed a few chapter members, and the next thing I knew, I was giving my first official tours. These guests offered trail maintenance tips, critiqued my proposed trail route, and pointed out various plants and trees that I had never really heard of, let alone identified. Luckily, none of them were hazardous. The initial results were in. People far more experienced and knowledgeable about trail building than me had declared this parcel of land an excellent place for a trail.

With less than a week before our big meeting, I made a trail. Mowing an initial path through the tall, overgrown grass took more time and gasoline than I had planned, but the result provided a sense of giddiness and accomplishment I had rarely experienced before. Now I needed a hiker, and I knew exactly where to find one. Watching my toddler daughter scamper along the trail, frolic in the wildflowers, and smile in the sunshine made all the work so far well worth it. I could only imagine how that joy would multiply with a whole class of explorers enjoying nature.

But first the director of curriculum and I met with Larry Kascht, director of the Retzer Nature Center, an environmental learning center operated by the county parks system. Even though Retzer was less than an hour away from where I lived and even closer to my school, I had never been there before. On that warm August afternoon, Larry's passion and knowledge about nature immediately showed. As we walked the trail, he pointed out anything and everything our five senses could experience in the outdoors. The only thing more palpable than his intelligence was his enthusiasm, which was contagious. Plus, hearing all the positive things he had to say about the current condition of the land was very encouraging. He noted the land's incredible potential and was blown away that it had remained in such pristine condition and hadn't been overrun by invasive species. I left the meeting with a huge sigh of relief and more excitement than ever before. I felt an instant connection with Larry and made plans to visit Retzer in the near future.

After the trail tour with Larry, I felt quite confident that my plans and proposal would be accepted and I would officially become an outdoor kindergarten teacher in a few short days. I tried to enjoy the fleeting moments of my summer vacation, visiting the trail often and visualizing the nature fun just days away. Then, just days before teachers would be returning for meetings and planning time, I received official district permission to use the space for learning. Named after our school's mascot, the Timberwolf Trail and Outdoor Classroom had become a reality. Now the real ride could officially begin.

Sort of. While I had official permission from the district, I was also informed that this permission was provisional, based on four conditions. Each one posed a potential pitfall. In fact, failing to meet the first condition would not only have ended the ride, it would have closed the entire park.

Condition #1 – If One Parent Says No . . .

My plan was approved just in time for me to start preparing my classroom and receive my class list. Traditionally, after receiving my class list, I send classroom parents a general letter introducing myself and previewing the upcoming year. But this letter would be different. The district requested (well, required) that my letter describe my plan for creating an outdoor classroom, with one teeny tiny caveat. Parents were required to "opt in." Essentially, each family had to agree to their child being in my classroom. I was told that if even one family refused to opt in, the program would not go on as planned. The district had no intention of switching students around, so it had to be a yes from them all. The fact that all my work and planning could have been washed away so easily added unanticipated anxiety. The roller coaster went barreling through a dark tunnel. After sending the letter to families, I waited. Then light appeared at the end of the tunnel. Everyone had opted in.

Condition #2 – Communicate Everything

The second condition involved communication. Before I did anything, and I mean anything, involving the land, I needed to let the district team know. Every student activity and outdoor lesson had to be documented and sent to the district. For the first few months, I sent dozens and dozens of emails, though it felt like millions. Before I removed thorny or low hanging branches, I emailed. Before I mowed, I emailed. Before I planned a hike, I emailed. Before I led a math lesson, I emailed. I also bombarded their accounts with short-term and long-term goals and possible ways to reach those goals. Eventually my communications either proved my credibility or got annoying. The district informed me that they trusted me and I no longer needed to be quite so communicative.

Condition #3 – Don't Ask for Money

When I shared with my district team some successful nature-based programs that were already in place around the country, they saw the positive effects a similar program could have here. However, they were also aware that the program could go the way of other initiatives and simply fade away. With the latter in mind, they let me know that no funding from the district budget would be used to support the program at this time. That didn't really bother me. At this point, I really didn't even know what I needed, so providing me with a budget would not have been very fiscally responsible. As I became more familiar with the program, I made a running list of potential purchases. Luckily for my own bank account and the success of the program, other resources would become available once word about the trail spread.

Condition #4 – The Experience Must Be the Same

This condition confused me. How could the children in my class have the same experience as in other classes throughout the district if my whole purpose of creating outdoor kindergarten was to offer a different kindergarten experience? I asked for clarification. It took a bit of back-and-forth before it made sense. The "experience" really boiled down to academic achievement and assessment scores. If the data points and test scores from my students were not up to par with everyone else's, the program would not move forward.

Guess what? Years later we are still moving forward.

Destroying the Box

6

A few days before the new year started, the school hosted a meet-and-greet event. The families came to meet their teacher and classmates, drop off supplies, and get a tour of the classroom. I didn't give tours of the trail, but I did answer many questions about it. I walked away from that night with a feeling that while the parents showed excitement about the coming outdoor experiences, they also wanted more information. My principal and I had a feeling the other teachers would want more information as well.

My colleagues have always seen me as someone who thinks outside the box. However, when introducing the trail and nature kindergarten concept to the rest of the class, I wanted to make sure my fellow educators knew this thinking outside the box was much, much more than simply bringing the box outside. Taking students outside meant destroying the box. In *The Playful Classroom*, Jed Dearybury and Dr. Julie P. Jones express a similar sentiment when they detail how "the proverbial box has one agenda: It holds us back" (p. 49).

The day before school started, we had one final staff meeting. We went over some logistical details and worked through a few team-building exercises. I must admit that my attention was not where it probably should have been that morning because I was mentally preparing for the afternoon. I would have the chance to share my vision with the staff right after lunch. First impressions are important, and I didn't want to screw this up. When everyone returned from lunch break, ready for a nap in the early afternoon lull, I stood in front of my colleagues and shared my ideas for my outdoor classroom. As I bantered and babbled my way through my prepared thoughts, something distracted me. The room that held our staff meetings has huge windows that show off the land I built the trail on. Earlier in the week, the director of curriculum told me that members of the district's lawn-mowing crew would be stopping by before the start of the school year to widen the path I'd created with my tiny mower. As I was wrapping up my talk to the teachers, I noticed some equipment arriving on the land but not on the cleared path. After my chat, the staff took a quick break, and I took an even quicker walk to investigate the events unfolding outside. I had enjoyed the coaster ride so far, but the repeated ups and downs had left me a bit queasy. That queasy feeling quickly plummeted into full-blown nausea. There was plenty of equipment on the trail, but none of it was mowing the grass.

When I designed the trail, I strategically placed entrances and exits to the trail, one on each end of the land and one in the middle. The projected trail meandered around certain special features I noticed as I became better acquainted with the area. The beautiful, mature oak tree was ideal for large-group gatherings. The seemingly endless blanket of goldenrod made the serpentine path I had mowed feel like a maze. The large boulders scattered around the land were sure to become favorite spots for the students. Located smack-dab in the center of the trail was the crème de la crème—a fantastic collection of fallen trees giving the impression they'd been intentionally placed there just for playing on. Visions of children climbing, laughing, and exploring the nooks and crannies of this area filled my mind. Appreciating how this area was so picturesquely perfect for a natural play area, I'd made sure the trail approached it from both sides. I was falling in love with the land. This fallen tree playground was my greatest love of all.

But now, this dream burst as every last bit of those fallen trees disappeared before me. Distraught, I could only watch as each one was chopped into smaller, more manageable pieces and removed. I went inside and contacted the district. Apparently, a final walk-through had deemed those trees unsafe. They were potential hazards because—I kid you not—*students might climb them*. Part of me wanted to yell out, "That's the point! They are *supposed* to climb them!" Feeling defeated, I wondered if everything I had tried to express about why I was doing what I was doing had missed the mark. Walking through the sawdust city that was supposed to be the highlight of my trail put everything into question. However, I knew I needed to use this as a teaching point, rather than react in any other way. To save the few fallen trees that remained, I realized I would need to provide education and explanation that detailed how the benefits of certain activities outweighed the risks. Starting a program like nature kindergarten requires teaching children in new environments *and* teaching adults in new methodologies.

When it really comes down to it, classroom design doesn't matter. Minutes are meaningless. Homework isn't worth the paper it is copied on. I could do everything imaginable to create the most student-friendly, differentiated, learner-first atmosphere possible, but if all I did was simply move my classroom outside, it would all be for naught. Even with the crown jewel of my outdoor classroom chopped down and hauled away, the possibility for incredible change was still at my fingertips. I had transformed my classroom into a play-based learning environment. I had an absolutely fantastic outdoor space just feet away from my building. Everything I had worked for was right in front of me. The district had been gracious and generous enough to trust me to do what was best for my students. Now, bringing my vision to life was up to me.

The First Year Outside

Being somewhat of a veteran teacher and able to reflect on my early years, I have joked that the first year of teaching is the easiest because you really don't know what you don't know. In my second year, I realized just how clueless I really was. My understanding of my actual teaching responsibilities had been completely lacking. For example, during my first year of teaching fourth grade, I held Fast-Food Fridays. Every Friday I chose a small group of students, took their orders from a local fast-food restaurant, and had my retired father pick up and deliver the food for our special lunch. Good for student morale? Sure. But it was financially draining and not the healthiest choice for developing bodies or Friday-afternoon sanity. My academic insights were not much better. In my rookie year, I'd brought enthusiasm and fun (and french fries) into the classroom, but I had missed the boat on a great deal of teaching. For example, by the end of my years of teaching fourth grade, I had worked with my team to develop an expansive, year-long unit on Wisconsin history loaded with engaging and memorable learning experiences connected to social studies standards. But back in my first year, I'd covered the Badger State's entire history in one afternoon using just one worksheet. That's right, I covered nearly four hundred years of my state's history in a single worksheet. Chalk it up to inexperience and a plain old lack of understanding of everything teaching-related.

I did not want to commit any rookie mistakes in nature kindergarten. During this first year, I would test my vision and see where the adventure took me. All my research and reading didn't hold a candle to real-world experiences. The thrills and spills of creating a nature kindergarten program had come to an end—nature kindergarten had arrived. Now the faster, more death-defying ride started to leave the station. The highs were higher. The lows were lower.

The twists and turns were edgier. The loops and swoops were intensified. And this ride has no end in sight.

Looking back, the first year outside is a blur. As with most days in kindergarten, what actually happened didn't always follow the script. Perception never quite meets reality when working with five- and six-year-old children. Anyone who has felt the joys and pains of working with this age group knows that everything (and I mean everything) can be a distraction. A pencil eraser. A streak on the floor. A noise in the hallway. The most mundane things turn into fascinating objects of discovery. Now imagine the distractions that exist outside, where Mother Nature is the designer. We accomplished half of what was planned in double the time. I remember feeling anxious about my class missing lessons I had planned when something else grabbed their attention. Now I appreciate how I'd failed during those anxious moments to capitalize on the power of inquiry present in those experiences in nature. Our first encounter with a woolly bear caterpillar took a huge chunk of time away from my prepared instruction as each child *needed* to hold our fuzzy new friend. I remember rushing students through the line rather than letting their natural instincts to explore and discover lead the way. Learning is never a straight line, but the literal and figurative meandering paths to learning on the trail were time-consuming and stress inducing.

But the children should never be blamed for mishaps along the way. That was on me. Even though I had taken my class outside, shaking off my old teaching style took me a while longer. I still felt the urge to plan every detail of our outdoor time. I still wanted to control the flow of the day. I created lesson and unit plans and tried to force Mother Nature to stick to them. I worked many, many hours creating an outdoor classroom year-at-a-glance form displaying how my lessons and units followed the seasons. Traditional lesson planning often gets mundane and monotonous, and being able to connect learning to outdoor experiences allowed me to plan and prepare outdoor activities with a renewed passion. But as passionate as I was, my classroom still lacked something. Eliza's warnings were being realized: my curriculum was disjointed and my outdoor and indoor classrooms were not in sync.

Filling My Plate

Inspired by Eliza's Forest Friday approach yet wanting to blaze my own path, I designated Wednesday as our nature day. I scripted activities and lessons according to seasonal themes and couldn't wait for every Wednesday so that my carefully cultivated plans could be realized. Initially, I'd felt I needed to be in as much control as possible in this uncontrollable outdoor setting. While I had changed the setting, I had failed to change other elements of my instruction. Though taking my classroom outside moved us in a better direction, I still felt lost. Our outdoor day felt disconnected and separate from the rest of the week. If creating a cohesive indoor and outdoor classroom could ever happen, I needed to push the envelope and think outside the box. As I implemented more and more nature-based strategies into my classroom, it became clear that I needed to destroy the box. Attempting to create cookie-cutter outdoor experiences thwarted the emergent learning happening in our outdoor classroom. Although my lesson plans were connected to the curriculum, they were denying students the maximum benefit of learning outdoors. Students needed to lead the way in our outdoor classroom, even if that meant going off trail, so that in turn, owning their learning in this way would spill over into our indoor setting. I feel somewhat embarrassed when I look back at how I taught kindergarten before I incorporated nature the way I do now. I had failed then to look beyond the academic needs of my students. I had done those students a disservice by ignoring what was best and instead settling for what was easy.

I needed another revolution, this time in my instructional implementation. *Instructional implementation?* Is that the newest educational buzzword? In less fancy language, it's what you teach and how you teach it. I needed an overhaul in both of these areas to become a nature-infused educator. As mentioned earlier, a condition for the survival of nature kindergarten depended on academic achievement and assessment scores mirroring those of traditional classrooms. I couldn't and didn't change the expectations and end goals of the curriculum. I could and did adjust the path to get there.

Before nature kindergarten, my plate was definitely full. But looking back, I find that much of what had loaded my plate was repetitive, unnecessary, and unhealthy. One of my kindergarten colleagues likes to say, "Work smarter, not harder." This couldn't be more apt. I needed to trim the fat and fill up my plate with as many of the healthiest items I could find. Healthy for my mind. Healthy for my body. Healthy for my soul. Most importantly, healthy for my students. Was I being mindful, or was my mind full? By reconfiguring the responsibilities on my plate, I found my plate was still quite full but much less overwhelming and with much more appetizing results.

When I considered how I might incorporate more nature into an already jam-packed schedule, I realized my play-based schedule must evolve even further. In the kindergarten world, the holy grail of scheduling is a required, and often rigid, literacy block that tends to be fixed in the morning hours because research suggests morning is the optimal learning time for early learners. Hence, maximizing their learning potential with mornings full of phonics, reading, and writing sounds logical. My old self followed right in line, living in the world of literacy until lunch. A sizable math block slated for the afternoon along with specials meant that science and social studies got the short end of the stick. My new self hoped to find a healthier, more flexible balance. I felt that the literacy block had wonderful merit, but sticking to that rigid requirement squeezed out essential minutes needed for other areas of instruction, particularly those often forgotten or carelessly compressed subjects of social studies and science. If I could gently massage more nature time into my indoor-day mornings, I could strengthen these forgotten subjects. Integrating nature into my traditional literacy block would support more meaningful and authentic applications of essential literacy skills. I decided to address both problems by utilizing resources based on social studies and science standards to teach literacy-based skills and lead various literacy activities during the morning literacy block so that we read, write, and experience science and social studies, rather than blindly trudge through scripted and repetitive curricula.

Case in point on the perils of scripted curricula: while piloting a prospective science curriculum, I taught the lesson as it was packaged, without supplementing resources like I usually do. One lesson focused on animal habitats. The animal chosen by the resources was the beaver. A very cool and interesting animal, but if you pause to think, you might guess where this story is heading. *Dam.* I am probably exaggerating a bit, but I am pretty sure this lesson uttered that word 217 times. Every other word was *dam.* On the grand scale of bad words, it is relatively innocent. But to kindergarteners, it is a big deal. When I previewed the lesson, I predicted it could be problematic, but when I taught it, I chose to follow the script and simply plowed through the lesson. I didn't think much about it until I received an email from a parent wondering why I was repeatedly cursing in class. Luckily, I extinguished that fire.

Working in concert with my curriculum changes, I revamped the classroom library, adding various fiction and nonfiction nature-associated books that were still applicable to reading-strategy instruction and writing standards. Using these books as mentor texts for student writing both modeled developmentally appropriate writing techniques and strengthened students' understanding and appreciation of the natural world. My students became much more engaged while practicing phonics, spelling, and writing strategies with words and concepts they had already experienced. I replaced traditional math tools used for counting, measuring, and patterning with natural items. Similar to when I had provided my students with more time to play and create, I saw improved focus and attention instead of the behavior issues and inattentiveness I'd witnessed with traditional instructional practices. Bringing nature into our indoor classroom created connections to the activities and experiences of our outdoor classroom, which united both settings and legitimized outdoor learning. Though obviously different, the outdoor classroom became an empowered place of learning rather than an escape from the monotony of a traditional indoor classroom. Did these changes take extra time, planning, and consideration? Without question. Would it have been much easier just to use the supplied curricular resources and regurgitate the lessons verbatim? Certainly. Do I see myself ever reverting to traditional curriculum by taking nature out of my instruction? Absolutely not.

Assess This!

Assessment. It's the educational equivalent of scrubbing the toilet, washing the dishes, or folding laundry. Nobody wants to do it, but somehow, some way, the chore needs to get done. And completing these assessments was crucial if I wanted to prove that my play-based and nature-infused educational approach produced academic growth and learning comparable to kindergarten peers in more traditional classrooms.

I'm not anti-assessment. I understand there must be some way to evaluate our students and our systems. In fact, you could even say I like assessments, as long as they're developmentally appropriate. And child-centered. And meaningful. And not too long. Or too much.

The beginning of the year feels like a sea of assessment, and the waves are anything but calm. The waves keep pounding and pulling you farther away from where you want to be—actually teaching. Just when you think you are about to reach the surface and fill your lungs, another wave flips you around. With the undercurrent of data pulling you below the surface, you struggle to keep up, eventually crawling back to land just in time to be drenched by one more breaker. You didn't quite drown. But there's no time to celebrate, since the next assessment tsunami awaits in the distance.

Now maybe that seems a little dramatic, but trust me, it's not. Imagine yourself in a kindergarten classroom of twelve to fifteen bright-eyed, bushy-tailed children eager to follow your every direction, listen to your every suggestion, and devote their undivided attention to every moment of your flawless and exciting instruction. Then, after you wake up from this dream, let's zoom in on reality. You have a room of twenty to thirty children acclimating to life away from home. They want to do well, but they don't know exactly what that means in this new and unusual setting.

Distractions abound. Academics aren't their highest priority. They want to eat snacks, need to use the bathroom, and wonder when they get to go home. Yet one of teachers' required tasks at the earliest stages of the year is assessment. Though we have letter sounds to teach, writing stages to advance, and reading levels to climb, we assess like our job depends on it, because in many cases, it does. To get where you need to go, you need to know where you're starting from. I get it. We do need to assess. But are we assessing in the most efficient and appropriate way that respects and protects children's developmental levels, mental health, and engagement?

Case in point: In my fourth-grade days, one of my higher-level readers was two questions into an online reading assessment. As instructed, she raised her hand when she needed assistance. When I got to her computer, she had an interesting question.

"What is *so crates*?"

I wasn't sure I'd heard her correctly, but she repeated the question while pointing at her screen. I was flabbergasted. Please tell me why a fourth grader would need to know anything about Socrates, the Greek philosopher credited as a founder of Western philosophy. I'll wait.

Still waiting.

Yep, still waiting.

It's very possible that question was an outlier. But even so, its presence made me wonder why. Why that question? Why this test?

Fast-forward to teaching kindergarten. This time five-year-olds were taking the math version of that same online test. Five-year-olds who have grown up with touchscreen tablets and smartphones. After teaching them that a computer mouse had nothing to do with cheese or long whiskers and explaining to them why they shouldn't touch the screens, the test began. Having been designed for five-year-olds, the test featured an automated voice that read out loud to the student each question and set of answer choices. Even though the students were reminded of this multiple times, many forgot. They were kindergarteners. Forgetting is about as frequent as breathing for some. Luckily, I caught them and turned on their sound. Most of them at least.

I noticed one of my students had finished this forty-two-question test in just twelve minutes. After asking a few questions to figure out how he'd done that, I realized that he hadn't really taken the assessment but had instead made a game out of clicking the mouse as fast as possible. Yet when I reviewed the students' assessment results, I saw that he'd scored well. Extremely well. Very surprising, considering he struggled to identify shapes and count past eleven in the classroom. The validity and reliability of this assessment was very much in question. Again I ask: why this test? I wish these were isolated incidents. I urge you to ask any teacher you know about assessment hiccups they've encountered, and I am sure you'll hear some real gems.

More important than these potential outliers are the anxiety and stress these assessments induce. In many cases, students stress about them because they have been trained that they *need* to be right and that these tests represent who they are. Many teachers stress about them because they *need* their class to do well because they feel that others value them as educators based on their results. Even administrators at both the school and district levels stress about them because they *need* to garner the community's support and they hope impressive assessment scores will accomplish that. Sometimes even parents stress about them because they *need* to feel validated as parents based on their child's success in school. Not to turn into Dr. Seuss here, but if the scores are more, will the stress be less? Can anyone even tell which kids test well? Are kids really the best based on a test? I could go all day, but I'd rather go play.

Terrible poetry aside, some assessments suck up fun and spit out frustration. Some are time-consuming. Some are repetitive. Some feel forced. Yet we know assessment is needed. But the real question shouldn't be *why* we assess, but *how*. So far you've read how I completely transformed my educational philosophy, from the way I schedule to the way my room is designed. And while I have made many changes, there are some things I cannot change. Whether required by the district or the state, some assessments are unavoidable. Between administering various tests required by the state, performing continuous district assessments, and managing repeated running records, you might think I should change my job title to *assessor* rather than *teacher*. Yet assessments help me form learning groups, identify strengths, and focus on areas of student and teacher growth. Like I said earlier, I do like assessments—if they actually help.

When I explain my classroom and the many projects and programs we dabble in, many people ask how I manage our time. Basically, how do we fit in the instruction and assessment I am required to complete while still leaving ample time for play and nature? The answer is simple. Don't separate these things. When you separate instruction and assessment from nature and play, getting everything done is impossible. It takes an observant eye, patience, and creativity, but using play and nature to develop your instruction and complete your assessments is a timesaver. Plus, when given time, space, and opportunity, students learn from their time in nature and play experiences in deeper and wider ways than any lesson or assessment I could plan on my own.

This doesn't mean I don't teach. I do. This doesn't mean I don't participate in assessments. I do. But I try to maximize students' ownership over their learning by minimizing the control exerted by required teaching and assessing. If this sounds confusing to you, don't worry. It was also confusing and difficult for me at first. I was an anxious assessor. Intentionally or not, as a teacher who worried about not fulfilling my curricular requirements and having students who were unsuccessful academically, I spoon-fed them information and taught to the test. But the learning felt forced and fake. Inauthenticity abounded as the product conquered the process. But as my teaching philosophy evolved, I realized that instruction and assessment do not have to be independent from nature and play. In fact, they work together quite nicely.

One awesome benefit to teaching in an outdoor classroom is that students learn constantly, often without even trying. While they learn by playing, I assess them by observing. In an outdoor classroom, learning is disguised as exploration and assessments are disguised as play. Emergent learning is now at the core of our classroom, and as a result curricular requirements are reached more naturally. Our experiences are authentic. Our learning is meaningful and memorable. But how do you assess in nature? What do you assess about play?

Play profiles. As mentioned earlier (see pages 46–47), play profiles are a documentation tool that connects play opportunities to report card indicators and early childhood skills. When given the chance, children can display all the skills and knowledge required of them with minimal adult intervention. Just listen, watch, and let the power of play take over.

Fallen tree. Assessing as children climb trees within the first few days of the school year yields very informative data in many domains. Besides the physical benefits, tree climbing "allows for emotional benefits, such as building confidence, helping each other, perseverance, freedom, sharing, peace, meditative, empowering, social activity, and self-awareness" (Gull, Goldstein, and Rosengarten, 2016). After briefly instructing the children in tree climbing, I set them free to explore our fallen trees. The district left behind three fallen trees that lie in close proximity to each other. One is a fallen log, another has a slight incline, which makes climbing it a tad riskier, and the other is our primary fallen tree, which is taller and features multiple limbs. It is always a class favorite. It doesn't take long for students' natural tendencies to emerge. I see rule followers and rule breakers. I see risk-takers and risk avoiders. I see those who show concern for others and those who are oblivious to the world around them. I see who is impulsive and who is cautious. I see leaders and followers. In just five minutes, I learn more about my students than I would from a week's worth of traditional assessments.

Hike leader. Once the class is experienced on the trail, I add the hike leader position to our classroom jobs chart. The title says it all. As long as the hike leader holds that position, he or she leads the hikes. They determine the route and control the pace. This may seem simple, but it is much more than just going for a walk. By observing how students lead a hike, I get a sense of what they like, what they avoid, and how they interact with peers. This information may seem unimportant at first, but how students improve their hiking endurance and leadership skills as the year progresses uniquely showcases their growth. To be a good hike leader, the child must understand the current situation, pay attention to the rest of the hikers, and take notice of things in their surroundings to point them out to others. A quality, well-led hike tells a great deal about that leader.

Bird feeder leader. One of our activities during spring is placing bird feeders. We use various styles to attract a diversity of birds, and one portable feeder is equipped with an attached camera. After selecting and researching birds that could visit the trail, each student creates a trail sign showing their bird and installs it along the trail. The sign provides information about the bird, including physical characteristics, diet, habitat, and fun facts. Students use what they have learned about these birds in the bird feeder leader assessment. Using the bird feeder equipped with a camera, each student puts the fully stocked bird feeder somewhere in our outdoor classroom. They write up a simple paragraph that tells which bird they aim to attract and why they decided to place the feeder in that location. Every day we check the camera, and then a new student places the feeder in their selected spot. The assessment isn't the actual feeding of the birds; it's the conversations before the child places the feeder, explaining their reasoning, and the conversations afterward, discussing the results.

Ticks and sticks. Ticks and sticks are two of the outdoor classroom's riskier elements. From early in the school year, we discuss ticks, share information about them, and even incorporate them into our class routines. For example, we add little legs to dice to create little ticks. Exposure to and experience with ticks lessens everyone's apprehension. The education even filters home and eases parental concerns. Similarly, we learn, practice, and share stick safety protocol. To test their knowledge, students teach other students and guests on the trail about ticks and sticks. Observing a student teaching stick safety and methods for minimizing ticks can tell a lot about their ability to retain and communicate information.

These assessments certainly don't fit any traditional assessment model. No ovals to fill in or answers to click. To students, they don't even feel, look, or sound like assessments. Yet disguised as play, they provide valuable information that extends far beyond academics. There are no traditional end-of-unit assessments or quarterly progress reports in nature kindergarten.

Nature kindergarten is all assessment all the time—assessing risk, assessing relationships, assessing responsibilities. Knowing this and deliberately paying attention provides an amazing array of information that goes deeper than any traditional test can. But since many assessments are required, like it or not, I will note that assessment scores in my classes have not dropped since introducing this play-based, nature-infused approach. While I still feel angst about assessing (and often overassessing) students, I know that the skills students are learning and practicing while engaged in play and immersed in nature will leave lasting imprints on their educational experience and build a sturdy foundation upon which they can continue to grow well beyond their nature kindergarten year. Children deserve assessments that don't judge them on what they know and what they have yet to learn, but instead develop their skills to become efficient learners, successful stewards, and responsible community members.

Outdoor Life

Now, I can't speak for other places, but Mother Nature gets quite confused in Wisconsin. While I absolutely adore experiencing the unique characteristics of all four seasons, when all of them occur in the same week it can be tricky. For example, my birthday is May 11. When I turned eight, my outdoor birthday party had to be canceled because of a late spring snowstorm. The following year had another outdoor party cancellation, this time due to flooding. The year after, we planned an indoor party because of the weather the previous two years. Any guesses on the weather that day? If you guessed seventy-five degrees with white puffy clouds and a gentle breeze, please pick up your prize on the way out. Some say Mother Nature is unpredictable. I prefer to say she's flexible. So I try to be flexible too.

This flexibility goes well beyond how I manipulate a schedule or design cross-curricular opportunities. This flexibility allows for, and sometimes requires, instantaneous decisions that alter the path of the day. If we're in the middle of a spelling activity and notice sandhill cranes out the window, we're going outside. If the schedule says it's math time but the rain that has been pouring down all day has stopped and rays of sun are peeking through the clouds, we might set out to do some puddle explorations or write number sentences in mud. And sometimes the little cherubs show a bit of rust on their halos and everyone would benefit from a break. We'll head to the trail and let nature open our minds for learning.

Daily doses and regular immersion in and with the natural world are key. Different schedules on different days affect the amount and timing of our outdoor excursions, but if we have school, we go outside. The time of year also influences our outdoor learning. At the beginning of the school year, we emphasize nurturing student relationships with the land and explicitly teaching and practicing expectations for the outdoor classroom. Just like scaffolding, the teacher initially holds more control in order to support children moving toward emergent opportunities. Once the class knows the outdoor classroom's boundaries and has shown progress in being safe with each other and nature, the amount of time spent outside increases, the areas we explore widen, and the students' freedom expands.

Then, as it does every year without fail, winter arrives. The temperatures drop. We play hide-and-seek with the sun, and the sun usually wins. The flakes fly. We are expected to slow down and stay inside. But we don't.

Those who dread the gloom and doom of winter's gray days do their best hibernation imitations by staying inside as much as possible. Nature kindergarteners view the coldest months of the year in a different light. They notice the crisp, clean air. They see the fresh blanket of snow as a clean canvas. The frigid frostiness doesn't intimidate them. While the actual minutes spent outside may decline, we still get out. Winter offers new ways to grow and learn that simply can't be replicated in an indoor environment. It's easier to stay inside. It's easier to complain about the cold and dreary conditions. It's easier to wait until the winter gear is stored away. But what's easy isn't always right. And what's right isn't always easy.

Nature kindergarteners choose what's right. They embrace the chill. The snowdrifts. The subzero temperatures. The air that literally hurts your face. Not exactly most people's idea of a good time, and certainly not what many would consider ideal conditions for nature play. But winter's wrath doesn't have to discourage outdoor exploration or nature play. Embrace the chill.

Whether winter play is correlated with healthier immune systems, increased exposure to vitamin D, improved mood, or strengthened muscles, the research is irrefutable—it is extremely beneficial for children and adults alike. Yet many avoid it. Maybe some don't like the monotonous and time-consuming process of gearing up. To others, a landscape blanketed in glistening snow doesn't scream beauty and adventure. Many others just despise the cold. Winter play is all about mind over matter. If you don't mind, it doesn't matter. And embracing the chill starts with preparation.

Planning starts well before the flakes fly. First is a shift in mindset. One must understand and accept the mantra "There is no such thing as bad weather, just bad clothing." Even the hardiest children struggle in winter without proper gear. The excitement of playing in the snow disappears as fast as a snowball in July once a child's hands get cold and wet. Cold is tolerable. Cold and wet is miserable. Waterproof gloves are a must, but other gear certainly doesn't hurt. Warm, waterproof boots are crucial when there's more than a dusting of snow on the ground. Snow pants are a great addition with or without snow. In fact, I like to call them *warm pants* because they are wonderful for any cold weather. Warm coats and breathable but cozy hats, scarves, and socks are also quite helpful. That being said, you want to make sure you don't overdress. You want to be able to move comfortably and avoid overheating, which can be a surprisingly real issue in winter.

Second, getting used to wearing all that gear is crucial. Practicing gearing up in winter attire while the summer sun is shining or the autumn leaves are clinging to the trees might seem odd, but trust me, building muscle memory through repetition goes a long way. Anyone experienced with young children can painfully attest to their struggles with zipping and snapping. Familiarizing children with the process of putting on gear in the correct sequence and moving around in it helps children become accustomed to it and lets the adults identify issues with it before they spiral into mountains of trouble.

A third (and probably most essential) way to embrace the chill is to spend time outside every day, especially as the temperatures begin to dip. Enjoying the outdoors on a bright, sunshine-filled day is easy. Committing to outside time when weather is not optimal takes a bit more practice. As winter approaches, those who shelter inside are destined to struggle when forced outdoors. Just like learning to ride a bike, practice makes progress. Simply put, the best way to master being outside in winter is . . . by being outside in winter. Get acclimated to the falling temperatures by spending time outside each day. You'll notice that regular trips outside automatically help you adjust to the changing temperatures. In doing so, you don't really notice that much of a change, and the bitter cold loses its bitterness.

Winter is on the way. You've got the gear. You're used to putting on and wearing the gear. Your stamina for the season is strong. You are ready to embrace the chill and enjoy nature play in winter. But how?

- *Search for animal tracks.* Grab one of the many delightful picture books on winter tracks. Then find and identify tracks and see what imaginative stories you can create based on your observations.

- *Go snowshoeing.* With various kid-friendly models available, snowshoeing is an excellent opportunity for winter exercise and discovery. Get out there and make your own path!

- *Build a mouse house.* Let your inner architect blossom as you design and build small homes with natural materials. Fill your homes with nuts, seeds, and berries, and monitor your visitors. Check for nearby tracks, or better yet, set up a trail camera and see which winter friends make an appearance.

- *Go birding.* Not all birds migrate. Grab some binoculars, find a comfortable space, and search for some fine feathered friends.

- *Create a color castle.* Using food coloring, water, and ice cube trays (or other freezer-friendly containers), create colored ice cubes. Take them out-side and construct your very own color castle.

- *Paint the snow.* Hopefully you still have some food coloring left after creating your colored ice cubes. Mix it with water in spray bottles or squeezable water bottles and make a snowy masterpiece.

Eventually spring returns, even in Wisconsin. By this time of the year, students are trail experts and naturalists in training, yearning to learn more. This beautiful marriage of knowledge and curiosity fits perfectly with spring, the season of new life. The melting snow and bursting buds symbolize a fresh start. Spring belongs to the children. Exploration and play define the essence of spring in nature kindergarten. Months of observing, journaling, discussing, and experimenting come to a head as we now spend almost all our time outdoors. The trees and flowers marching toward maturity match the path these students take on their nature kindergarten journey. Coming into the year, the students were newly hatched birds. They were hungry for knowledge but mainly had to rely on others to "feed" them. As they grew and changed, they developed their own interests and abilities and started to venture out of their nests. Eventually, like the avian fledglings we observe and monitor, the students spread their wings and took flight.

"Nature's Dozen"

Even before the first year of nature kindergarten was in the books, we could deem it a success. Based on the results of family and student surveys I sent, random emails I received, and word of mouth in and around the school community, the outdoor approach I introduced to my school was extremely well received. Parents appreciated having such an innovative experience in their community school. The school and district eagerly declared my approach successful so they could use it as promotional fodder. However, teachers were . . . well, let's just say the buzz and excitement felt by families and other community partners wasn't as intense among the teaching staff. Teachers know that when someone else starts a successful program, positive pressure is probably coming their way to adopt it too. Understanding this, I had already taken various steps to make that positive pressure more palatable for any less-than-enthusiastic colleagues.

I had been using—perhaps abusing—email to share ideas and information with my fellow teachers about taking classrooms outside. Regardless of the resource, I shared information incessantly. I hoped these email updates would encourage others to get outside and take a hike. Literally. The momentum nature kindergarten had set into motion needed to continue. I didn't want outdoor opportunities to be an afterthought. I didn't want other teachers to see time in nature as an obstacle to learning. I didn't want these changes to be viewed as difficult. I aimed to share ideas that were manageable, meaningful, and simple. I kept track of the tips and tricks I shared throughout the year and created a document I titled "Nature's Dozen." For your enjoyment, I have included them below, in no particular order.

1. Start small. *The journey of a thousand miles starts with one small step.*

The idea of taking a classroom of children into the great outdoors can be daunting. Not every teacher is overly excited about the possibilities nature has to offer. Whether it is fear, inexperience, anxiety, or another factor, someone can always find an excuse to stay in their comfort zone and remain within walls. Growth, however, does not come from standing still. Risk creates opportunity, and with every opportunity comes potential. Therefore, risk creates growth.

Taking the classroom outside starts with a single important yet simple step: going outside. Maybe a walk. Maybe a read aloud. Maybe a science observation. Maybe a math lesson. Increasing experience in the outdoors goes hand in hand with increasing appreciation for the outdoors and an increasing appreciation for *using* the outdoors as a classroom.

2. Change locations, not expectations. *You don't have to recreate the wheel— just change the direction it takes you.*

Once your mind is open to taking the classroom outdoors, starting slow and sticking with what you know can be easiest, so do outside what you do inside. Both students and teachers can benefit from easing into the outdoor learning experience. Stick to the already familiar lesson plan and let nature be there to support the learning. As a teacher gets more familiar with the distractions, excitement, and apprehension of going outside, they can better prepare for sustainable outdoor experiences.

3. Make it a routine instead of a reward. *Nature is a right, not a privilege.*

School and routines go hand in hand. Teachers tend to be creatures of habit. Making outdoor experiences routine alleviates issues due to inexperience and cultivates innovation. Comfort in an outdoor classroom requires time. Inversely, using outdoor time as a reward inherently eliminates the outdoor classroom's credibility as a place to learn. Allow the outdoor classroom to be an extension of the classroom, not an entirely separate entity.

4. Roll with Mother Nature's punches. *There's no such thing as bad weather, just bad clothing.*

Inclement weather should not stifle learning or keep students inside. Both weather and the results of weather can and should be used for learning, unless the weather is hazardous. Spending time in all sorts of weather creates unique learning opportunities. Obstacles are opportunities in disguise. As with most everything else, being prepared is essential. Weather's drawbacks are minimized when you mentally and physically prepare for it. If it's wet, write or draw with mud. If it's snowy, search for tracks. Dirt doesn't hurt and water will dry.

5. Be a proactive problem solver. *Turn a problem into a possibility.*

Knowing that the outdoors can be unpredictable, you will be wise to be proactive in your preparations. For example, knowing that both children and adults may feel anxious about ticks, you can teach students about the bugs to minimize that fear and increase everyone's level of comfort. By introducing the concept ahead of time, incorporating it into the classroom, and providing real-world information and strategies, you can lessen the children's fear of ticks. In fact, finding a tick can become a rite of passage. When the students' fear and anxiety decrease, their families' fear will follow suit. While you can't prepare for everything Mother Nature throws your way, you can and should take the necessary steps to try.

6. Expect and embrace the unexpected. *Learning can come when you least expect it.*

Some of the most meaningful and memorable educational experiences come when you least expect them. Flexibility is key. Let nature be the teacher. Intentionally allow for play and exploration. Release the tight grip on control and let students take the lead outdoors. This facilitates a more personalized and engaged learning environment in which twenty-first-century skills like communication, critical thinking, collaboration, and creativity can thrive.

7. Bring nature inside. *Mother Nature is the best teacher.*

Bringing nature inside can be done both literally and figuratively. Bringing natural items into the classroom for hands-on exploration and use with lessons is always acceptable, especially when weather or other factors inhibit true outdoor exploration. Incorporating natural items in place of typical classroom tools can be as easy as providing sticks and leaves for making patterns instead of counters or pattern blocks. Similarly, teachers can easily incorporate nature into their instruction. Use a book on trees to review text features. Determine the area and perimeter of a garden. Debate the importance of pollinators versus the risks of bees. Nature can and should be connected to the curriculum and cater to real-world, authentic experiences.

8. Emphasize emergent opportunities. *Power to the young people.*

Student interests are varied, and engaging an entire class at once can be tricky. However, nature offers a multitude of equalizing opportunities. Children are naturally inclined to connect to the outdoors. When students are given the time, space, and opportunity to experience nature, they assuredly display interests and abilities in ways that may have been hidden in a more traditional setting. Teachers can observe their students' interests and engagement to improve instructional interactions with them. Personalizing the educational experience for children and allowing their interests to lead instruction will foster both deeper connections to educational standards and higher levels of engagement with the learning process.

9. Use your time wisely. *Work smarter, not harder.*

Teachers struggle with a lack of time every day. Many feel they have no time to plan. No time to grade. No time to breathe. However, research shows that going outside is a stress reducer.

In fact, taking the classroom outside can actually improve time management. Cross-curricular opportunities are easily intertwined in outdoor learning. Speaking of time management, research suggests that spending time outside helps students improve their ability to focus as they release pent-up energy. When students release energy, they grow in their ability to focus their minds and attention, which you can really feel when they return to a traditional classroom.

10. It's all about relationships. *Show your vulnerabilities so they can show theirs.*

Students look up to the adults in their life. We teach them so much more than the curriculum. Sometimes, taking time to breathe and relax is essential to cultivating a safe and comfortable learning environment. When teachers step out of their comfort zones, they show their students that they have the freedom and safety to do the same. *Relaxing* responsibility does not mean lowering expectations; it means taking time to focus on relationships. The relationships between teacher and students. The relationships between student and student. The relationship between school and home. The relationship between students and nature. Using nature to build and strengthen relationships offers unique learning opportunities that just don't exist if we rely solely on the curriculum.

11. Work hard. Play harder! *Children cannot bounce off the walls if we remove the walls.*

Play is not easily defined, but it is the ultimate differentiated instruction. Though play means different things to different people, one thing researchers agree on is that play is essential to development. Play *is* work. We all need it. Children deserve play. Lots of it. When you combine key elements of play and nature, you have a perfect marriage. Nature and play offer whole-child developmental opportunities, and believe it or not, academics are heavily strengthened through play. We are built to play and built *through* play.

12. Let kids be kids. *The power of play should lead the way, inside and out.*

Through it all, we can't forget that our job is not merely pushing kids through the educational system. We are here to improve the future. While this may sound like I'm up on a soapbox, it is true, and more important than anything else in this book. It is our responsibility to provide every opportunity for each child to be the best they can be. We must not penalize children for being children. Rather, we should allow children the opportunity to be themselves. Play is the way.

Trudging Along

My "Nature's Dozen" document is just one resource I provided to other educators during my program's first year in hopes of encouraging them to embrace outdoor learning. I invited other classes to come outside and see nature kindergarten in action. Better yet, I asked interested classes to be trail buddies with my students, heading outside together for various activities on a regular basis. I even went so far as to offer up my precious prep time to take other students outside, with or without their classroom teacher. My kindergarten teacher teammates responded to these opportunities by grabbing the bull by the horns—a level of enthusiasm that would be necessary as the program expanded in year two to include their classrooms. Other grade levels lacked the same enthusiasm, although I did receive occasional nibbles of interest. Many had questions. Some shared positive experiences they'd had on the trail with their classes. Students from other classes approached me to share that they had been on "my" trail. I am always quick to remind them the trail is for everyone. I want the whole school community to feel the trail is theirs, because it is.

When I realized that some teachers didn't share my enthusiasm, I have to be honest, I felt disappointed. I took it personally. When the outdoor learning space I had toiled to create for everyone went underutilized and even ignored, I felt slighted and insignificant. However, while that disappointment could've crushed me (and at times it did), more often than not, it motivated me. My confidence in outdoor learning inspired me to keep trudging along, often in the muck, to become a resource for my school community. Working tirelessly to take my kids out as much as possible, I hoped my passion for outdoor education would inspire others to follow in my footsteps, even if they started with baby steps. Rather than telling them how to get outside, I had to show them. That said, I couldn't force anyone to do what they didn't want to do. I just had to hope it would happen naturally.

During that first year, I definitely felt some uneasiness and tension among my colleagues as I purposely made waves in our systems and methodologies. A visit to the school board meeting in February didn't necessarily calm the waters. At this meeting, I, along with a few parents, gave a presentation about nature kindergarten. We discussed logistics, shared stories, and described how time spent learning and playing in nature benefited the students. As I listened to the parent portion of the presentation, I was humbled by their positive comments. The waters started getting choppy when a board member asked a parent if she wanted to see more outdoor opportunities for her children beyond nature kindergarten. Without a pause, she firmly and unequivocally responded with a statement that made me feel at once both proud and paranoid. She said that *every grade level needed to do the same thing*.

Gulp.

As the positive word about nature kindergarten got around, I began feeling some not-so-positive pressure from colleagues. Some teachers felt that nature kindergarten's success might force them to do more than they really cared to do. As soon as those words left the parent's mouth at that board meeting, I felt nervous about how fellow teachers might react. But I also wanted to give that parent a humongous and heartfelt hug for having the courage to stand up for what I feel is so important for children. As I had hoped, the program I started was moving forward and influencing my school beyond my classroom. I knew successes in some areas influenced decisions and opportunities in other areas. In other words, because parents were happy with nature kindergarten, the school would need to look at similar ways to keep them happy beyond kindergarten.

The Four P's

The biggest change in my teaching world was the philosophical transformation I underwent that first served as my catalyst for creating nature kindergarten, then blossomed through my first several years of the program. This philosophical shift transformed me.

Many educators are familiar with the four C's: communication, critical thinking, collaboration, and creativity. These are considered essential skills for success in the twenty-first century, and many schools have created initiatives to teach to the four C's. As my colleagues know, I'm a glutton for alliteration, acronyms, and wordplay in general, so of course I adapted these to my own philosophy, which I call the four P's. The absolute beauty of the four P's is that my nature-infused strategies not only increase the application of the four C skills but also add many more developmentally appropriate and developmentally important abilities. Let me introduce each of my four P's separately, showcasing how each of them builds from and extends the four C's and why each is crucial to whole-child development. While I will focus most intensively on how the four P's are used in our outdoor classroom, please note that our indoor classroom mirrors these techniques as well.

Play-Based

If you haven't figured it out yet, in our classroom everything revolves around play. I'm passionate about play. I like to talk about it. All the time. A wise man once told me repetition is the mother of understanding, but I'll do my best not to repeat too much here from previous chapters. But like teaching, I may fail, and that's okay.

From day one in a new school year, children receive multiple opportunities to play. I observe and participate during play. The students and I discuss it together afterward, highlighting things we noticed, both positive and problematic. This discussion leads to writing a play contract, an agreement that all students and I sign. Because play means different things to different people, we come to terms of play that the entire classroom can agree on and adhere to so everyone feels safe and respected. We refer back to this contract throughout the year and review and revise it as needed, especially when creative kindergarteners design new ways to play. Though the need and desire to play is inherent in all children, play is continually taught and practiced in both our indoor and outdoor settings. Play is a part of every day, and I wouldn't have it any other way.

We especially feel the power of play-based education when we head outside. Some of the constraints and limits that are necessary within the classroom walls disappear in our outdoor space. For example, students who are introverted or timid in the classroom often feel more free on the trail, and others who struggle with expectations inside the walls of the school may find success and happiness when they step outside. Like the late, great nature-based educator Erin Kenny often said, "Children can't bounce off the walls if you take away the walls." Nature is a great equalizer.

- ❏ Need to improve focus? Play in nature!
- ❏ Want improved coordination? Play in nature!
- ❏ Have excess energy? Play in nature!
- ❏ Struggle with fine-motor skills? Play in nature!
- ❏ Need to practice emotional regulation? Play in nature!
- ❏ Hope to strengthen current friendships and build new ones? Play in nature!
- ❏ Aiming to offer your students every possibility to grow as learners, friends, and community members? Play in nature!

Mountains of research prove that there should be no debate on the value of nature play in healthy whole-child development. During presentations, I often refer to nature play as play on steroids. It takes the positive benefits of play to the next level. Playing in nature won't automatically solve every problem or instantly make everything better, but the research doesn't lie. Playing in nature improves skills necessary for academic success, self-regulation, and executive functioning, and it is tied to improved health and increased happiness. But before jumping into some serious nature play, four factors need to be considered.

The "Unstructured" Fallacy

When I say play in nature, I don't simply mean adding more recess, though that wouldn't hurt. The fact that many schools have opted to take away recess bit by bit bothers me. The use of recess as a motivator for students to complete work and improve behavior annoys me, but punishing children for less-than-desirable behavior or incomplete work by taking recess away from them infuriates me. In my opinion, recess is a right. I feel the same way about play and time in nature. My play-based philosophy emphasizes emergent play. Adults are there to observe and assist as needed but should generally aim for a hands-off approach.

Emergent play is often synonymous with unstructured play, but I feel the word *unstructured* is misleading. Observant adults will appreciate the structure that exists in "unstructured" play. Nature play is not uncontrollable chaos—in fact, it is quite the opposite. When children are leading, nature play has intense flexibility and organization, even though the untrained adult eye might initially see it as a free-for-all. Rather than use the erroneous term *unstructured*, try *emergent* or *child-led*. A tweak in terminology can go a long way. Similar to scaffolding in a traditional classroom, adults can participate in and guide nature play alongside their children. As a child becomes more experienced with their environment, the adults can lead less and observe more. Once a child has accumulated an array of nature play experiences and subsequently earned the trust of their caregiver, they should be allowed the freedom and right to become the director of their own play. To me, this is real play. It isn't forced on children or watered down to avoid risk. It celebrates risk and promotes problem-solving opportunities that provide children the power and trust to compromise, troubleshoot, and resolve issues that may arise.

Risk vs. Hazard

Everyone must understand and value risk. Frequently considered a dirty word in education, schools often try (and fail) to eradicate and eliminate risk in the name of safety. But if you ask me, safety requires risk. Let me explain. Risk is everywhere. It's impossible (and irresponsible) to eliminate every risk for children. In my opinion, risk is necessary and its benefits far outweigh any drawbacks. Adults understandably feel the need to protect our children. But even with the best intentions, paving the way for every move a child makes does not equate to protecting them. In fact, sometimes it can prove the opposite, because when children grow up overly protected, their instinctual ability to assess and avoid true hazards becomes compromised. By nature, children are risk-takers. They intentionally seek out risk, even in the structured and organized plastic playgrounds so commonly seen in parks and schools across the country. Taking away children's ability to take risks by bubble wrapping everything may actually lead them to pay less attention to their play, thus leading to carelessness and ultimately more injuries. Research suggests that children get injured in these "safer" playgrounds *because* the element of risk has been taken away. For example, children who fall on the soft, spongy surfaces of today's playgrounds never experience the consequences of falling. Besides interfering with a child's understanding of safety, eliminating all risk within play can also eliminate their creativity, challenge, and discovery. Without appropriate opportunities for risk, children may engage in unsafe activities that move right beyond risky to hazard-ous to get the sense of adventure their bodies and minds crave. It's that sense of adventure that we take away from children when we "protect" them with "safer" playground equipment.

Adults often undervalue a child's self-assessment skills. Children should be able to use a challenge-by-choice strategy to own more decision making and control over how they use their bodies. Having children choose the challenges they are comfortable with provides them multiple opportunities to assess themselves and track their individual progress over time on a schedule that fits their developmental needs. With some simple expecta-tions, guidance, and obser-vation, both teachers and caregivers can help children regain crucial risk assess-ment skills so they can learn how to avoid hazards and hazardous actions. When adults step back, children step up. Putting trust back in the hands of the children is the best way to provide a true play-based learning environment.

Appropriate Risk	Unsafe Hazard
easily identifiable by children	difficult to assess
approached with basic understanding	lack of awareness
within child's control	out of child's control
growth is an outcome	harm is caused

Misunderstood Magic

Dirt. Water. Weather. I call these the three misrepresented elements of nature play. Unfortunately, adults who are attempting to be pro-active problem solvers sometimes inhibit the magic of nature play by purposely avoiding these elements. Children like getting dirty, and believe it or not, dirt and mud offer health benefits. Remember, dirt doesn't hurt. Water play can be risky, but water will dry! It also offers a prime example of understanding the difference between risk and hazard. Playing in perfect weather is ideal, but nature play in all weather encourages new perspectives and instills apprecia-tion for everything nature offers us.

Having parents on board for a play-based classroom is helpful. Teaching and communicating the expectations of a play-based classroom is essential. This is even more important when much of the play is outdoors. Dirt, water, and weather can be huge obstacles when parents don't trust or understand the value of nature play. In nature play, there will be plenty of fun and learning. There will also be mud, crud, and blood. Families' stress and frustration about extra bandages and loads of dirty laundry can be minimized by keeping everyone in the loop about the whys and hows of nature play.

To Pick or Not to Pick

Children (and adults) like going off trail to explore. Experiencing nature off trail invites sensory experiences that bring play to the next level. Children love picking flowers. They treasure trail blazing. They enjoy experimenting with a branch's flexibility. Going off trail is memorable and meaningful, but it is also controversial. Do the risks of going off trail outweigh the benefits? Are there hazards? Is the area in question ecologically vulnerable? Will the actions and activities associated with going off trail leave lasting ecological impacts on the land? When you are playing outside of your own yard or space, the expectations of that location must be respected. With some common sense and some basic education in respect-ing the environment, going off trail is an excellent element in responsible nature play.

Responsible nature play is not simply opening the door and sending children outside until the streetlights come back on—it is a collaborative effort between children and adults. When these four factors are understood, practiced, and practiced again, children will once again be trusted to climb trees, catch critters, and live life under the guidance of Mother Nature and their own imaginations.

Place-Based

Children are asked to take in many facts in various subject areas during their time in school, yet years later many of those facts—learned through rote memorization and drill-and-kill strategies—vanish into thin air. Think back to your early childhood and elementary school days. What do you remember? If you are anything like me, you don't recall specific lessons or test answers. I remember kickball and four-square battles on our blacktop playground. I remember decorating my desk with photos I cut from a magazine to promote the professional wrestling fan club I created (which had three members at its peak). I don't remember why I got my first pink slip (my school's behavior referral form), but I remember getting my second one for forging my dad's signature on the first. The only thing I remember related to academics is creating an audio book report on Beverly Cleary's *Dear Mr. Henshaw* with MC Hammer's hit *Pray* playing in the background while I retold the story. I'm still boggled at that choice.

Long story short, most of us don't remember *what* we learned as much as *how* we learned it. With so much information crammed into our brains day after day after day, much gets lost in translation or forgotten. I think it isn't really memory loss, but *memorization* loss. One way to combat this memorization loss is to focus less on memorization and engage more in memory making by providing authentic learning experiences that build from what children experience in life outside their classroom walls. A place-based approach attempts to do just that.

Children enter school with a general knowledge of the natural world in their own backyards and neighborhoods. While the amount of time children spend in nature may be declining, most

still have a basic understanding of the plants and animals outside their homes. Deepening my students' understanding of this hyper-local flora and fauna is a prime example of how I use place-based techniques. Posted on our classroom walls and celebrated out on our daily hikes, we embrace the actual names of the plants and animals. Beyond basic identification, we investigate how natural phenomena interact with each other. Defining and digging into our ecosystem helps children better appreciate and sustain it for the future. Whether identifying birds through birding, naming animals photographed by our trail camera, or differentiating among the various wildflowers and native plants that pop up throughout the school year, students who learn about and experience the diversity of life in one setting can mirror that engagement in other settings. Parents are often overwhelmed by the responsibilities of adulthood and therefore may not have the time and ability to be mindful about the changes in the natural world that happen in their own community. I am always excited and inspired when I receive messages from parents sharing how their child is teaching them about plants, animals, and the intertwined relationships that exist in their own backyards.

At the end of the year, being able to name plants and animals is certainly not a requirement and technically not all that important. It doesn't matter one iota to me if a child can't distinguish between goldenrod and bergamot. I don't lose any sleep if a child confuses frogs for toads or cranes for herons. Having hands-on experience with nature and building a better understanding of the ecosystem and community they are part of takes precedence over memorizing facts.

Place-based learning also involves direct engagement between students and the community. Students learn about and are actively immersed in opportunities that influence their personal lives. This engagement instills in them the power and pride of knowing they can and do make a difference in their community. For example, over the past handful of years, my classroom has forged a partnership with Children's Wisconsin, formerly Children's Hospital of Wisconsin. Some students were already aware of Children's Wisconsin because they or someone close to them had once been patients of the hospital. These past experiences helped my students, as well as their families and the broader school community, eagerly share and participate in this new partnership.

I hope that what my students experience in our community collaboration with Children's Wisconsin gives them the hope and belief that with hard work, effort, and creativity, they can make a positive change in their community. This in turn shows each student that not only are they an important member of their community, but they are responsible for making it a better place.

Project-Based

Many adults remember creating dioramas or decorating posters in elementary school to demonstrate their final understanding of a unit with some sort of visual aid. So when I mention project-based learning, these dioramas or posters may come to mind. But my type of project-based learning is totally different. It focuses on input instead of output—process over product. Through projects incorporating citizen science, service learning, and community collaboration, nature kindergarteners focus on learning outcomes that keep them engaged and intrigued while promoting sustainability and continued involvement for years to come, thus instilling in them the qualities of a lifelong learner. Whenever children feel inspired to personally invest their time and energy, they recognize they are a part of something bigger than themselves, and this leads them to better understand their role in a larger community. Nature kindergarten is meant to be just the beginning. Curiosity is piqued but hopefully hasn't yet peaked.

When you think of citizen science in education, early childhood may not seem like a natural fit. However, when students learn background knowledge about a topic, involving them in authentic opportunities that enhance and enrich real-world research through citizen science is extremely beneficial for even the youngest learners. Moving away from cookie-cutter lessons and scripted curricula to incorporate such opportunities may seem daunting. But can you think of a better way for students to learn about the world around them than to be directly and actively involved in it? Many projects apply skills from literacy, as well as other curricular areas, and support child development. Our classroom is involved in a variety of citizen science projects. Some are more hands-on than others, but they all allow children to participate in authentic research that accumulates data in order to make decisions that influence the future. Their future. Here are brief descriptions of a few of these projects.

Snapshot Wisconsin is a volunteer-based program led by Wisconsin's Department of Natural Resources (DNR). Volunteers are trained to set up, monitor, and decipher data from a trail camera. The program aims to observe the land in every corner of the state by encouraging landowners and schools to host their own trail cameras. We usually check ours at the beginning of every month. Initially, we focus on animal identification. As the seasons change, we notice how our photos likewise change. Are we seeing more animals? Fewer animals? Different animals? Why or why not? These photos spark discussion on topics such as migration, hibernation, predator/prey relationships, and ecosystems. As students notice patterns through the progressing year, they improve both their power to predict and ability to explain these patterns. Photos of fawns in spring set us up for studying the life cycle, a staple of our spring instruction. Even though most of our photographs feature repeated species, the anticipation of potentially capturing a new animal always excites the crowd. Students also love seeing animals in action, whether in flight, with food, or with offspring. These photographs provide children with new opportunities to widen and deepen their understanding of the natural world.

Birding requires patience and time—two things young children aren't exactly known for. However, with practice and persistence, kindergarteners can become avid ornithologists. Though we see birds around our school all year, our main study of feathered friends starts in January. This might seem an odd time to begin a birding unit, but the solitude and serenity of our cold Wisconsin winters makes this the perfect time for us. We start in the classroom by reading books, watching short videos, and investigating artifacts. While researching bird topics such as nests, beaks, feathers, and migration, we zoom in on a bird specific to Wisconsin and study it in closer detail for a few days at a time. We find and post pictures of the bird, practice identifying its call, and then create some sort of keepsake to help us remember it before moving on to another. Some years the keepsake is a bird trading card, modeled after the sports card collections of my youth. Sometimes we design signs of each bird and place them along our trail. No matter the method, consistent exposure to the birds we are most likely to see in our community cements them into the memory banks of our budding birders. Before long, with all of the photographs, artifacts, and arts-and-crafts projects, the classroom transforms into an aviary.

This indoor avian work is all building up to our main project: participating in the Natural Resource Foundation's Great Wisconsin Birdathon. During the Birdathon, groups raise funds to support priority bird conservation projects and go birding to identify as many different birds as possible. Because we do a great deal of upfront work practicing bird identification in the classroom, my students start watching for birds even before the Birdathon officially begins. On a side note, I always get a bit giddy when a student stops in their tracks to notice a bird outside our classroom window or reports birds they saw at home. We practice birding, slowly building up to about fifteen minutes of relative silence searching for birds, using only our fingers to point out any activity we notice. Fifteen minutes may not be a huge amount of time for the experienced birder, but for kindergarteners in the months of April and May, this is an eternity. Rather than complete our official observations in a single sitting, we spread them out throughout the two months during which the Birdathon occurs. With clipboards, pencils, and observation checklists in hand, we head out to different spots along the trail to tally the birds we see and hear. The Leopold-style benches located near bird-nesting boxes around the trail transform into birding stations. We discuss our observations and add to our list of correctly identified birds. It is wonderful to go out at different times of day in different weather and at different locations and then discuss how these differences affect our sightings. Building up patience, endurance, and predictive power, birding with children provides skills well beyond basic bird identification.

Expanding on birding, our nature kindergarten has joined forces with our county's new citizen-science initiative, Conservation in the Parks. Using volunteers, this initiative educates citizens about conservation by planning and promoting hands-on citizen science opportunities in the community. When this opportunity came to my attention, I jumped at the chance to volunteer with my own family. At the nature conservancy at the end of our block, we help out with a variety of projects, including monitoring wetlands and nesting boxes and completing surveys recording the local snakes, turtles, small mammals, and dragonflies we see. I also brainstormed how I could modify these projects for my outdoor classroom. We have no wetland, so that was out. However, we have plenty of bird-nesting boxes and a prairie in the midst of restoration, so I knew my students could support related community conservation efforts. We monitor nesting boxes, catch and tag monarch butterflies, and capture small mammals and insects to keep track of the creatures that visit or inhabit our trail and outdoor classroom.

Plants play an important role in our citizen science as well. One of the first topics we study is trees, specifically the beautiful oak trees spread around our land. Students learn the parts of trees, their life cycle, and their importance in a healthy and thriving ecosystem. As children become junior ornithologists, they likewise become junior arborists, learning how to identify and protect trees and other native plants. Each student also finds their own best-friend tree, or BFT, which they regularly visit, chat with, and hug, meanwhile learning about the important roles trees play in our ecosystem. They learn that plants everywhere need sun, soil, space, water, and air. We dig into these needs both figuratively and literally, adding trees to our forest and native plants to our butterfly garden and restored prairie. Through this process, we learn about three of our least-favorite topics in nature kindergarten: weeds, nonnative plants, and invasive plants. Weeds are plants found in an undesirable location, or the wrong plant in the wrong place. Nonnative plants are plants that originated from another area of the world. More specifically, invasive plant species are nonnative plants that harm the success of native plants in the area. As we review plant needs, we explore how these three types of plants cause problems for our land and negatively affect our ecosystem.

But nature kindergarteners don't just identify problems; we work to solve them. One way we solve the problem of invasive plants is by participating in a citizen-science project known as the Garlic Mustard Pull-A-Thon, hosted by the Southeast Wisconsin Invasive Species Consortium. This organization promotes citizen involvement in removing invasive species through education and fundraising in a competitive format—the team that pulls the most garlic mustard even wins a trophy. As my students become better versed in knowing what plants need, they come to understand how some plants help and others harm. Though garlic mustard is a harmful plant, it is both relatively child friendly and easy to identify and eradicate. It is easy to spot and, unfortunately, much easier to spread. We do some simple research in the classroom over winter, then keep our eyes open once the green returns. The sooner we find garlic mustard, the sooner we can get rid of it. For the citizen science project, we weigh our collection and add up our total amount pulled. The competitive spirits of the kindergarteners love seeing that total rise. That competitive drive is strong enough that families send me pictures and emails detailing how their child spent hours pulling garlic mustard from their own backyard, the local park, or their grandma's yard. They let me know how their child is identifying garlic mustard ad nauseum as they drive down the road. They inform me that their child teaches them about the plant, why it should be removed, and how it emits a stinky smell when pulled. Even though my class won the 2020 Pull-a-Thon—and the extravagant trophy that accompanies the title of Garlic Mustard Pulling Champions—the real prize was the stewardship and learning they gained through the experience.

While citizen science is a huge element in our project-based classroom, service learning might be just as important. I want my students to leave kindergarten taking care of one another and our world. Service learning opportunities on our trail showcase this belief through action. These stewardship opportunities nurture students' love and appreciation of the environment, sowing the seeds that bear the fruit of environmental responsibility for years to come. My students use the trail daily, and therefore they have a responsibility to take care of it for future users both from our school and from the wider community. Some service work focuses on maintaining the trail while other service work aims to improve it. All service work emphasizes taking action to improve the world and community. We complete seasonal trail work throughout the year. In fall we plant trees to diversify and increase the trees on our land. During dry parts of winter and in spring, we add wood chips to sections of trail that need tread repair. In late spring, we add native plants, remove invasive species, and thin out overly aggressive or bothersome native plants. Student stewards help set the table for an environmentally conscious and responsible next generation.

Service learning and whole-child development are one and the same. While serving others shapes and strengthens each participant's heart and soul, it also supports physical development, establishes confidence, introduces new opportunities, and instills pride and accountability. When I began including my kindergarteners in service learning tasks in our outdoor classroom, I worried that the work might be viewed as too far of a departure from the curriculum. However, once I saw how service learning boosts so many developmental areas and how it stays with students beyond the school's walls, I overcame my initial hesitation and now eagerly pursue more service learning opportunities for my classroom, inside and out. Watching the children take ownership of these activities gives them a wonderful sense of gratification and accomplishment. It does the same for me.

Citizen science and service learning projects involve and inspire both students and families. Every year, the children and their families report how their involvement in these projects leads to future actions that go above and beyond what is requested. The extra time spent on weekends pulling garlic mustard. The extra trips to the trail to show a family member or friend the outdoor classroom. Random bird identification on a drive home from the grocery store. Citizen science and service learning do more than enrich the curriculum—they also enrich the individual and the community.

Researching resources and seeking support for nature-based and environmental education has also connected me with other nature enthusiasts from other corners of the community. We refer to them as our "nature friends." Biologists at the county and state level have shared their expertise, joining us throughout the year to provide instructional support in our classrooms, inside and out. A prairie expert taught us about prairie restoration and led us in installing a butterfly garden and restoring a prairie. We've invited guests from the International Crane Foundation in Baraboo, Wisconsin, to share their knowledge about beautiful and fascinating cranes. We've hosted author visits with various authors who have written about nature and wildlife. Volunteers from local organizations, including the Ice Age Trail Alliance and Wild Ones!, a native plant group, have enhanced our program. We have also been fortunate, as a number of student volunteers from scout organizations have visited to improve the outdoor classroom, adding birdhouses, nesting boxes, storage crates, and benches for seating. And many individuals I've reached out to on social media and people from our school and local community have left their marks on nature kindergarten by donating their time, talent, and treasure.

One of nature kindergarten's favorite nature friends is naturalist extraordinaire David Stokes. Multiple times a year, he enriches our program with visits that include music, sign language, hands-on activities, artifacts, and humor. His passion for children and nature is both evident and unwavering. My wife and kindergarten team all joke that I am just waiting in the wings to be his apprentice, but I'd feel like a rookie stepping in for a hall-of-fame quarterback. I don't need that kind of pressure. Nature kindergarten is all about community. It truly takes a village.

That village would be quite incomplete without support from my students' families. Sending a child to kindergarten can be a difficult transition for both child and parent. For many, this is their first time being away from each other for the whole day. Any kindergarten teacher knows the feeling you get when a child approaches you and asks if it is time to go home . . . at ten in the morning. Being at school all day is a big deal. And a tiring one. Parents may experience a similar feeling of emotional exhaustion as they entrust an unknown teacher, and in many cases an unknown school, to take care of their child all day long. Then, when they come to realize that a significant chunk of that day will be spent outdoors "in the wild," parents may understandably have reservations. I have been fortunate to have parents who displayed more excitement than anxiety. They have questions, like any reasonable parent should. *How do you keep the whole class safe? Do you go out when it rains? Is there a bathroom out there?* But the families have been open to the program when their child is starting kindergarten, and they become excellent advocates for the program when the year comes to an end. This support goes well beyond appreciating and promoting the program. Parents deal with the intricacies and details of an outdoor classroom, which often go above and beyond the expectations of a traditional kindergarten classroom. Remember, there will be mud, and there could be blood. On top of the extra supplies, incorporating citizen science and service learning often adds extra requests from school to home, such as asking families to go birding and share their results for our Birdathon project or donate some time after school or on the weekend to help with some trail maintenance opportunities. And more often than not, families step up to the plate and knock these requests out of the park.

Personalized

In my opinion, personalized learning is about trust. Trust that spending time in nature builds essential skills. Trust that observing and holding back from intervening benefits children. Trust that allowing decision making to transfer from teacher to collaborative partnership to the children themselves is necessary and helpful. Trust that the children can and should be the leaders and directors of their own play and their own learning experiences. Trust in each child.

Play-based learning relies on this trust. Imagine sending a classroom of five-year-olds out in nature for child-led, unstructured play without trusting them. That would be dangerous and unprofessional. When people hear about what my students do in nature kindergarten, they often imagine a crazy or chaotic scene. I love to challenge that theory by inviting them to experience it for themselves. The best way to win over skeptics and teach others about the outdoor classroom is to invite them in. Then they can see and feel for themselves how time in nature and nature play is much more than just students releasing energy. They see that it takes time and practice, just like any other skill. They feel the excitement and engagement. They also better understand why providing this opportunity for children is a collaborative process and a powerful technique for personalizing learning. The time spent learning about the outdoors, identifying risks and hazards, determining physical and emotional boundaries, and experiencing the land together is necessary to building trust.

Besides the very personalized power of play, students in nature kindergarten become their own decision makers, guiding their learning in their indoor and outdoor classrooms. For example, before I infused more play and choice into the classroom, I taught students through learning stations in the classroom. These stations included about a dozen to fifteen activities centered around a theme or two, and students rotated through each activity in pairs. Literacy skills dominated the stations, though I occasionally incorporated art, fine motor practice, and strategy games. Though students could choose from some differentiated options, each worked through basically identical stations, regardless of ability level, learning style, or interest. While students worked independently, I pulled some into small groups for word work, phonics, or guided reading. Students worked in their stations for twenty to forty minutes, depending on the time of year. If they finished early, they read books from their guided reading bags or the classroom library. Essentially, students had little to no choice. And it showed.

Rule followers followed the rules. Those who struggled with independent work continued to struggle. Many rushed, making careless mistakes. Some avoided work altogether. This comedy of errors led to repeated do-overs, wasted instructional time, frustration, and crushed confidence for both students and teacher. This wasn't good for anyone. I realized that personalization was imperative. First, I changed how I grouped stations. While some activities were designed more for pairs or small groups, I allowed for more flexibility in how and where students completed their tasks. I also gave students more opportunities to choose their station, though I did have a say in some groupings based on the availability of supplies and resources. For example, if we only had access to two computers, I chose two students rather than allowing a first come, first serve scenario. Additionally, when a student struggled with a skill and needed extra support, I worked with that student in a small group or one-to-one meeting to discuss and practice that particular skill before assigning them to a specific station. That method was used infrequently and only when I felt the lagging skill could have a detrimental impact on future learning or student confidence. Second, I began offering a more diverse selection of activities rather than limiting choices to literacy-based games and worksheets. I included familiar strategy games. Science activities and extensions from our class lessons were added. I put more time into station selection and implementation, based on student needs and student interests. Lastly, I provided more freedom of choice for students once they completed their work. Rather than getting a secondary assignment after they completed their main task, students chose from a menu of options. Whether it was art, free reading and writing, games, quieter toys, or visits to the loose parts library or classroom nature center, choice became an essential component of stations because it allowed for true creativity and independent learning to flourish.

Did these changes boost the overall success of station time? Without question. More engaging options and choice increased student engagement, meaning fewer students avoided working. For my part, this change proved to be a timesaver—no more scrambling for fresh and gimmicky activities every month. Incorporating activities from other curricular areas made everything more familiar and gave students a more active role in selecting and completing their work. Including curricular-connected activities along with developmentally appropriate activities involving art, fine-motor skills, and strategy games strengthened stations by eliminating busywork and emphasizing whole-child learning. Students took more ownership and control over their decision making. Based on the work students chose, I made more informed and personalized educational and planning decisions. I gained a better perspective on student interests, the type of work they avoided, and the work that needed to be included in our smaller groups—forming overall a more global perspective of each child. In a nutshell, changing my stations improved my understanding of my students, and I could use that understanding when guiding them to being the best learners, friends, and community members they could be.

I tend to tell others who are thinking about taking their classroom outside that a nice way to start is to do what you normally do, just do it outside. If I were true to my word, I needed to do this in my own teaching. So I did. Changing learning stations sparked a new initiative that took off like wildfire: outdoor stations. Following a similar format, students chose from various curricular-connected, whole-child activities around the trail. Different options develop over time, as students increase their skills and build familiarity with the trail. In the beginning of the year, I foster independence by including work-alone practice with review activities. Some students work in one area of the trail with books about selected topics. Others make letters with sticks. Still others practice numerical order using labeled rocks. As the year progresses and our trust and skill sets grow, so do the responsibilities and choices available to the class. Winter may seem like a time of limited choices, but whether it is snow painting, winter tracking, snowshoeing, or good ol' nature play, winter is a busy time for outdoor stations. But spring is when the year of effort, decision making, and growth comes together. Students know the trail and their outdoor classroom like the backs of their hands. They have acquired a wealth of experiential learning, creating personal comfort and curiosity with the natural world. They also have nearly a school year's worth of experience with self-directed play and learning opportunities. That experience, combined with their understanding of the social and behavioral expectations, makes spring the perfect time to literally and figuratively let them run free and let their actions speak for themselves.

Citizen science and service learning also support personalization as students participate in activities like pulling garlic mustard and spreading wood chips on the trail, which benefit both their outdoor classroom and their own development. They also have other options that rely on personal choices, independent actions, and individual interests. One station opportunity invites students to observe a nesting box and jot down what they notice. This becomes especially popular when we know eggs or chicks are in the box. Students also work with a portable trail camera. They place it near a bird feeder, nesting box, or structure they have made, often sprucing up their selected area to attract visitors. Checking the camera the next day is a highly anticipated event.

Digital cameras are also available to the children. Teach a child to fish and they'll never go hungry, right? Well, teach a child how to use a camera (and get past the selfie stage) and they'll never get bored. Their unique perspectives produce incredible images. Their explanations of their selected photographs give me insight on where they find beauty and inspiration in their outdoor experiences. Cameras also heighten the joy as students record their nature play. While initial excitement about the camera can be distracting and make things a bit dicey, the shine eventually wears off and the true experience of play is documented. Observing how children play is a remarkably eye-opening way to appreciate their growth. Another outdoor station option is nature art. While some art activities are teacher guided to allow students to expand on past projects, some of the most amazing pieces of nature art are created independent of adult instruction or intervention. Children's creativity takes over when they have the time to independently select their materials, elaborate on their ideas, and construct their own creations. For example, using a wooden lobster cage donated by a teacher, the kids once created a wood store with wood chips as currency. Students brought unique pieces of wood to the store, and other students bought and bartered with them, alternating between shopkeeper, workers, and customers. During any outdoor station session, it would not be too far-fetched to see students reading books, observing nest boxes, nature journaling, mud painting, pulling garlic mustard, and climbing trees. It's all in a day's work in nature kindergarten.

The four P's represent so much more than play, place, projects, and personalization. They are the essence of my classroom, inside and out. They represent my desire to provide a well-rounded,

whole-child educational experience that helps children reach and exceed academic expectations while building on foundational skills necessary for future success as students and individuals. Regardless of test scores or reading levels, students leave kindergarten with a love of learning and a desire to do their best for themselves, their school, and their community.

Time to Grow Up

9

I have always loved nature. Spending time outside recharges my batteries. However, loving nature doesn't make you a nature expert. You might think a person who created a nature kindergarten program would know a lot about nature. I guess that all depends on your definition of "know." I knew that I didn't know everything. In fact, compared to other nature-based educators I had forged relationships with, I knew very little. This became very clear in my outdoor adventures with my kindergarteners. More often than I'd like to admit, when students asked me about something they'd found or seen on the trail, I simply did not have answers for them. It all worked out because a core element of outdoor learning is inquiry. Inquiry allows for students to be curious, which helps them design their own paths to understanding rather than simply receiving answers and moving on. Despite this, I needed more credibility in my nature knowledge, especially since I expected that there would be pressure to expand our program's reach and I would be the main contact for that expansion. If I hoped to be the leader of any outdoor educational movement in my district, I had to be less of a nature novice and more of a nature expert.

Inexperienced Expert

As mentioned earlier, spring is a time of exponential growth. If I too were to grow as I expanded my outdoor program, I would need support, and I knew just the man to help me. The time to reconnect with Larry Kascht had arrived. Since our first meeting at the trail, I had visited the Retzer Nature Center a few times. Occasionally I'd run into Larry. We exchanged pleasantries and discussed the progress of the nature kindergarten program, and his courtesy and genuine interest impressed me. Seeing his seemingly innate ability to relate to the natural world solidified for me how much I needed to improve my own knowledge. I was enthralled with his enthusiasm and expertise and figured he would be the perfect person to help me upgrade my nature interest into nature intelligence.

Retzer Nature Center offers many programming options for schools, extracurricular groups, and the general public. Though naturalists on staff lead these programs, the center also relies on trained volunteers known as Retzer teaching naturalists, or RTNs. After learning about and connecting with some of these RTNs, I decided to become one too. Not only would I deepen my nature understanding, but I would better acquaint myself with program ideas and resources I could adapt to nature kindergarten. After conferring with Larry, he personally trained me as an official Retzer teaching naturalist. Over several training sessions, we read about nature, talked about nature, and experienced nature. Larry and I also chatted about the goals for each of our own programs. We shared similar visions for getting the next generation into nature, so it seemed like we could each be a piece in the other's puzzle. While Larry sought to increase relationships with schools, I hoped to add credibility and viability to a blossoming outdoor kindergarten program. Working together, we could support each other and strengthen both of our programs. It seemed like a perfect symbiotic relationship. During one of our final training sessions, Larry led me on a brief tour of the planetarium attached to the nature center. Not to get overly cheesy, but I couldn't help but feel the stars begin to align. Every time I came to Retzer, my affinity and appreciation for it grew. Investigating how it could play a role in nature kindergarten's future made perfect sense. With the future in mind and knowing that positive pressure had already spread to other classrooms, my conversations with Larry morphed into collaboration.

One of our goals involved developing and sustaining community relationships. Larry and the Retzer Nature Center wanted to move past a simple field trip model and build lasting relationships with schools. Larry and I decided that the best way to build on the success of my individual classroom was to start a partnership with the entire kindergarten team. We set a schedule to meet eight times over the course of a school year. Half of the visits would be at the nature center. The remaining visits would occur at our school's trail. These visits would follow the seasons and allow for experiential and meaningful activities in both a traditional classroom and out in nature. Using existing programs from the nature center's list of offerings, Larry and I created specific curricular connections for each program along with post-program activities to enhance the experience. We also adapted the programs so they would intentionally build from each other to deepen natural connections and strengthen social relationships between students and naturalists.

Clearing Hurdles

On paper these plans seemed perfect. But for a successful collaboration, plans are just one piece of the puzzle—we also needed money. As my college economics professor repeated every lecture, "There is no such thing as a free lunch." While Larry's nature center loved hosting students, they also needed financial compensation for their programming and staffing. Larry would give us the best prices available, especially since this collaboration supported the center's goals. However, knowing that the district had already communicated its funding constraints (don't ask for money!), I needed to get creative to make ends meet.

I didn't exactly beg, borrow, or steal, but I came close. In the program's first year, I spent much more than I care to admit to create the trail, maintain it, and furnish supplies for our extensive array of outdoor activities. I tried to minimize these costs by purchasing from the dollar store, but I also relied on other sources. Requesting supplies from families is an option, though one that I tried to use

sparingly. I told my story on social media and essentially begged for supplies. During regular trips to my municipality's yard waste collection site, I may or may not have borrowed stumps and sticks from its mountains of yard waste. I also received some stumps and wood from my Ice Age Trail chapter's maintenance manager. To enhance my indoor classroom, I added a nature center full of treasures like shells, rocks, bones, and feathers. A simple email to local taxidermists produced various artifacts that likely would have been tossed away otherwise, including elk teeth, turkey feet, and oblong deer antlers. I took advantage of every opportunity and exhausted every option to enrich both indoor and outdoor environments.

One unexpected benefit of creating the trail has been the community partnerships born from this process. During nature kindergarten's first year, three simple emails I'd composed to gather support and supplies for the trail each led to community connections and partnerships that have become staples of this program.

Back when I was considering creating the program, I'd sent my first email to investigate grants offered by our district's education foundation. The foundation's director responded by requesting a face-to-face conversation, so I invited her to the trail and shared my short- and long-term visions for nature kindergarten and outdoor opportunities throughout the district. While she was enthusiastic about this exciting and potentially groundbreaking opportunity, she asked that I hold off applying for grants until the program was a bit more established. As the initial year progressed, I kept that in mind and waited for the perfect opportunity to reconnect with her. That time presented itself after Larry and I crunched numbers for the potential kindergarten-wide collaboration. After telling my kindergarten team about my desire to apply for a grant, our proposal application turned into a formal presentation to the foundation's board. Shortly after our presentation, we received the good news. Our grant was accepted and fully funded. In year two, nature kindergarten would expand to four kindergarten classrooms.

While I was extremely pleased to receive funding to cover the cost of eight nature center experiences, we were not allowed to use grant money for transportation costs. Ordering buses gets quite pricey. The kindergarten team wanted to keep nature kindergarten economically feasible for our families, so we had to be creative to keep costs down. To make this happen, I wrote my second email. This one went to our school's parent-teacher organization. Seeing value in what we had already done and what we hoped to do in the future, the organization's board immediately approved covering our transportation costs. Now all four kindergarten classrooms would experience a one-year collaboration with Retzer Nature Center without families paying a dime.

As nature kindergarten developed, so too did the trail's design and layout. With our nature center collaboration expanding to four classrooms, the trail would definitely be used more. I needed to create more large-group spaces for outdoor classrooms along the trail. It was time for my third email. It went to a number of local tree service companies, explaining our nature kindergarten program and requesting stumps and logs to create larger group areas. I received only one response, but it was all I needed. It came from a family-owned tree service company whose owners had children in the district. When I shared specific details about what I needed, they instantly agreed to help. Even though their children attended a different school, they believed the program would benefit the district. Through their generosity, the trail received much more than just a few logs and stumps for seating. During that first year and every year since, they have unselfishly donated wood for a variety of projects. Logs and stumps to upgrade seating options. Wood chips to improve tread. Tree cookies for all sorts of curricular uses, including end-of-the-year keepsakes. But the most impressive donation was unique and special wood pieces to expand our trail's natural play area: supersized stumps for tables, smaller tree trunks buried in the ground for seats, and some stumps even carved into tree thrones.

Broadening Our Horizons

With the expanded collaboration, all kindergarten classes would receive more outdoor opportunities. I spent countless hours smoothing this transition for my teammates as much as possible. I provided a lengthy list of nature-related books. I created a year-at-a-glance form detailing how nature could be infused into our already-packed curriculum. I shared integrated, cross-curricular units. They appreciated this groundwork I laid for them. They demonstrated responsibility in their questions, insight in their perspectives, and creativity in building on what I had begun. Truly, the program moved from being *mine* to *ours*.

As we started the second year, we had two options. Start small or undergo baptism by fire. Trusting my team could handle it, we got baptized together. We walked away a bit smoky but were never fully engulfed by flames. Our full-team experience began the same way I start every day—through play. Watching twenty-five kindergarteners enjoy hands-on experiences in nature is invigorating, but watching over one hundred of them on the trail is mesmerizing. To get everyone better acquainted with nature kindergarten, teachers hosted natural play sessions. Each of us monitored an area while the students explored their outdoor classroom. These sessions forged strong relationships between students, teachers, and the land. As we observed students collaborating, problem solving, and displaying creativity during these play experiences, we received immediate insight into students' personalities and the power of being outside.

My amazingly flexible and innovative team trusted my vision and understood my passion. They knew my intention through everything was to support whole-child development. I can't express how grateful and fortunate I am that these excellent educators trusted me and took risks with me as we embarked together on this outdoor adventure. However, we certainly couldn't have done it alone. Nature kindergarten could have easily gone the way of the dodo bird if not for many, many generous and supportive advocates. Building a nature kindergarten is an incredible amount of work, but when that work is shared among an amazing system of contributors, it makes the load much more manageable.

Appreciating our great success in expanding nature kindergarten across the entire grade level in year two, we continued our "baptism by fire" mentality as we prepared for years three and beyond. After discussions with administration and grade-level representatives, our school pursued an all-school Retzer Nature Center collaboration. Coordinating a collaboration with a school of over six hundred students was daunting, to say the least, and it would have been impossible had the nature center not offered much-needed support. Faithful director Larry Kascht suggested that the Friends of Retzer, the nature center's friends' group, might be willing to help financially. Larry spoke very highly of this group, and it didn't take me long to find out why, as they responded promptly to my initial contact with immediate approval and a generous donation. After securing this funding and expanding the grant from our district's education foundation, our school collaboration was fully funded and prepared to broaden and deepen our influence on our entire school community. But now that my dream of building an outdoor program in my public school had become a reality—and a successful one, at that—I had to keep the momentum going. The school district wanted to do its part, so it

www.youtube.com/
watch?v=E5qNYmDsMi0

decided to showcase our outdoor program on its web-site. Students from the high school's audiovisual club joined us on the trail for a number of weeks to make a promotional video for the program, documenting activities and interviewing students. The video not only helped celebrate and validate the immense work and planning that had gone into developing the pro-gram; it also provided momentum that would help the program expand into the future.

To this point, my work increased outdoor opportu-nities for my students, school, district, and community. But of course, I wanted more. To share how my success story could be adopted by other schools, I took my show on the road and submitted presen-tation proposals at various play, nature, and education conferences. I was given my first opportunity to share my nature kindergarten program outside my school's walls at a regional nature-based early childhood education conference. My presentation slot fell right after lunch. I left the meal early and brought a plate of food to the presen-tation room to snack on while I made sure my slideshow was loaded up properly. As attendees started trickling in, I gobbled down one more bite of juicy pineapple. Maybe it was nerves or perhaps depth perception issues, but I quite literally bit off more than I could chew. I chomped down on the end of my fork and chipped a front tooth moments before presenting to a room full of educational profession-als. The tooth ended up being a very minor dental issue, but it started my professional presentation career off on a rather chippy note.

I've now presented at various conferences around the country and, surprisingly, I still have a full set of teeth. Presenting still stirs up butterflies in my stomach, though, whether I'm in front of child care providers, district administrators, or anyone in between. With adults I know, I speak loudly, tell terrible jokes, and use physical comedy to keep things loose (ask to see my high kick). But in settings with peo-ple I have never met, I'm quite shy. Forcing that introverted self to come out of its shell and share my story can be intimidating. When I first started presenting and saw so many knowledgeable and pro-fessional people, I started to feel like an inexperienced expert again. I loved nature and working with kids, but being around others who shared my passion for getting people outside cemented the fact that I wanted and needed to learn and share so much more.

Onward and Upward

The first two years of nature kindergarten were wildly successful (pun intended). As we prepared for year three, we could proudly look back on our first years. The trail had transformed into a working classroom. We had new funding partnerships. Our community collaborations had been created, then strengthened. The kindergarten team had laid the groundwork for a hopefully seamless transition to including higher grades and employing established scheduling and programming tips and tricks along the way. I was excited about the bright future for outdoor education at my school. Some shared that excitement. Others did not. That positive pressure trickling upward brought out some not-so-positive emotions that had been festering. Opposition to expanding nature kindergarten into other grades bubbled to the surface. Teachers who thrived on control didn't appreciate disruptions to the routines they'd worked hard to set in place, while others didn't feel connected to nature-infused learning. Still, I believed in the idea and was willing to champion it. I'd heard from many parents who wanted similar opportunities for older children. My principal supported the initiative and was pleased that I had secured funding to include the rest of the school. He and I always knew how positive pressure could affect our school. After two years and one successful expansion, we felt the school was ready for another. Boy, were we wrong.

All Aboard

Ask my wife. Ask my team. Ask me. I'm pretty dense. I don't always catch on to things. However, when my principal announced at a staff meeting during the planning days of year three that, like it or not, all grade levels were joining the nature center collaboration, the silent-yet-thunderous stares of my colleagues spoke volumes. I already knew change would be hard for them, especially when they were "voluntold" to accept it. However, when a teacher I work with closely and greatly respect told me it wasn't fair that I'd pushed my passion onto her, something hit me. Part of my work must be to clearly convey that what drove this initiative was the program's benefits for the students, not simply my own interest. While I knew this would be an uphill battle, I definitely underestimated how steep that hill would be. Better start climbing, step by step.

Knowing that some staff weren't thrilled with their unexpected involvement in the schoolwide collaboration with Retzer motivated me to make it as easy for everyone as possible. Reminiscing on my days as a conductor on Milwaukee County Zoo's miniature locomotives, I did anything and everything, from ordering buses to designing programs, to get everyone aboard the outdoor learning train. I put tasks on my plate to lighten others' loads and hopefully ease their tension. Like the previous two years, I offered prep time to lead activities and invited other classes to be trail buddies. I got a little interest but mostly crickets. I decided to try something different and go smaller. At a committee meeting focused on specific behavior interventions, I suggested that students who needed an extra relationship boost or a break from the traditional classroom could become "trail experts." Before long, my class had an additional trail expert from other grade levels joining us just about every day.

Cleverly or annoyingly, depending on your feelings about acronyms, I told the staff that everyone needed a little H.E.L.P. Breaking it down, going outside can be as simple as taking a *Hike*, *Exploring* an area, *Learning* about something there, and *Playing* in nature. The suggestion didn't sweep the staff off their feet, to say the least. But I'm not one to give up. I shared that concept with teachers from the district's other elementary schools, and in year three, I hosted a number of classes from other schools. Timber Trips was born. The name had a nice ring to it, considering that our mascot is the timber wolf and our outdoor classroom is known as the Timberwolf Trail. I also presented outdoor ideas to the district administration team, offered professional development sessions on play and nature at both district and school levels, and visited each district building to assess each school's possibilities for implementing nature-infused opportunities. During those visits, I fell in love with a small, forested area surrounding our combined high school, middle school, and intermediate school. I connected with a high school teacher who was interested in using the forest for outdoor learning and shared my tips and tricks for working with administration. Before we knew it, the district had a second nature trail and an absolutely gorgeous outdoor space that offered quite a different ecosystem from the Timberwolf Trail. Together this teacher and I brainstormed possible district uses for the newly created trail. Nature kindergarten definitely took advantage of it, meeting our friends from Retzer Nature Center there twice a year.

In my own class, we set up a Forest Friends pen pal program with a nature-based kindergarten class from Vermont. On a monthly basis, we exchanged friendly letters, sharing information about our personal lives and our indoor and outdoor classrooms. The program culminated at the end of the school year with a virtual visit online. My class also used the virtual world to observe live animal cams from all over the world and connect with nature experts from our local community and beyond.

Slowly but surely, my school's staff were opening their eyes and minds to the benefits of infusing nature into their classrooms. Still, I aimed at minimizing their work as much as possible. Taking over the planning of a schoolwide collaboration physically exhausted me at times, but it inspired me to keep thinking big. Luckily, I had Janet Barthel, Retzer's new fearless leader, by my side. Janet had taken over supervising the nature center upon Larry's retirement. She had previously been second in command, so she was already involved in our collaboration. Her enthusiasm, encouragement, and knowledge about Retzer's programming options helped streamline an all-school plan that diversified the environmental experiences and transitioned in a logical and constructive manner.

I also leaned on my personal experience in leadership and development. For years, in addition to leading the Ice Age Trail's Tyke Hike program, I'd taught Saunters, a summer school hiking class in my district. In cooperation with the Ice Age Trail Alliance, Saunters brings students to the Ice Age Trail to introduce or deepen understanding of topics like glaciation, physical wellness, and resiliency. I added another weekly session, opening up spots for more children to hike. I also developed Operation Explore, my own outdoor summer school class, which is essentially nature kindergarten compressed into two weeks. It offers nature play, citizen science, service learning, and so much more. To keep the momentum going, I started the WOLF nature club. Short for Woodside Outdoor Learning Families, WOLF is a family nature club that holds monthly events at one of our district sites or out in the community. Initially aimed at my own school, Woodside Elementary, it has since expanded to include the entire district.

With the outdoor initiatives I had brought to my school, district, and community, I hoped the winds of change would blow away the academic-first mentality like a tornado. It felt a gentle breeze instead. But at least the air was moving.

Pumpkins for a Purpose

One element of my four P's approach involves building awareness that each child can positively influence their community. Our relationship with Children's Wisconsin exemplifies this. Our collaboration now involves various events and activities throughout the entire school year, but we started much smaller back in year two of nature kindergarten.

Excited at the prospect of developing this collaboration with Children's Wisconsin around our Wants and Needs unit, I couldn't wait to get started with unique and engaging activities for the class. The unit's timeline fell between Halloween and winter break. After differentiating between wants and needs, the class earned Dargatz Dollars at school, which could be spent to purchase *wants* like extra recess, play days, treats, and so on, or donated to Children's Wisconsin. Though the class did spring for a few *wants*, they donated significant Dargatz Dollars to the hospital. (Using an exchange rate, I turn their donated dollars into real money.)

I get bored doing the same thing, so each year I add a new twist. First, I allowed Dargatz Dollars to be earned at home. Then I introduced Giving Contracts students could choose to sign—a promise to give up something from their holiday wish list and donate its value to the hospital. Walking the walk, I likewise asked families to refrain from giving me a traditional teacher gift and donate instead. As much as I love Dr Pepper and Swedish Fish, the hospital needed help more.

The students even came up with their own ideas to raise money. One year a few decided to sell hot cocoa in their neighborhood, akin to a summer lemonade stand. This sparked the creation of our annual *Cookies for a Cause*. Using cookies donated from school community members, the class hosted an afterschool bake sale with all proceeds supporting the hospital. Students talked about the project and passed out posters and flyers about the hospital, so every transaction included a sweet treat and awareness about Children's Wisconsin. Just like the leftover cookies, this event left us hungry for more. Its success made me wonder how our outdoor classroom could take this collaboration to an even higher level. Since a staple of our daily schedule is a trail hike, I thought we could use the idea of hiking to add nature into our collaboration with the hospital and created *Pumpkins for a Purpose*. We invited families out on the trail, which we'd decorated with harvest and Halloween-themed items. The hike also offered nature-related and seasonal activities, including leaf collecting, nature paintbrushes, selfies with a scarecrow, and of course, a pumpkin patch. Waiting at the end of the trail were treats and a request for donations. The school community supported our inaugural event by donating treats and decorations. When the big day arrived, decorations filled the trail, treats proliferated, and our pumpkin patch was a veritable sea of orange. As luck would have it, frigid temperatures and some of the year's first snowflakes joined us that unseasonable October morning, but they didn't stop brave pumpkin pickers from visiting the trail and donating over $900. Our first nature-infused collaboration project was a chilly success.

We then created a second outdoor event, *Recycled Art Gallery*, scheduled for the week of Earth Day in late April. Once *Pumpkins for a Purpose* wrapped up, we started collecting recyclable materials. Bottle caps. Milk jugs. Tin cans. We took it all. We spent time every week researching items, organizing supplies, and creating pieces of recyclable art. Some of our favorites were bird feeders made from two-liter bottles, pictures of flowers and trees created from discarded puzzle pieces, and a big igloo that we could actually sit in made of gallon milk jugs. We intended to host our inaugural art sale in our outdoor classroom around Earth Day and donate all proceeds to the hospital. Unfortunately, a global pandemic altered our plans. Now that it looks like school is back in session, a closet full of bottle caps, tin cans, and milk jugs are waiting to be transformed.

Full Circle

Sometimes even the longest journey ends up exactly where it started. Many Saturdays during the school year and throughout summer, you will find me on the trail. I am in charge of maintaining it, but I also go there for myself. Being there physically refreshes and mentally rejuvenates me. But one balmy Saturday afternoon, I wasn't there for me. After a morning of mowing and tidying up the trail, I welcomed a few nature kindergarten graduates back to their outdoor classroom. Together we discussed our afternoon plans as we awaited our guests, a busload of nature-based education enthusiasts. As part of a nature-based preschool conference in neighboring Illinois, participants took a field trip to several sites. The Timberwolf Trail was the third and final stop of the Wisconsin field trip day. Knowing where the attendees had already visited earlier in the day, I felt I had an almost impossible task to keep them entertained and inspired.

If you've never been to Milwaukee, you're missing out. The city's original planners designed an array of amazing parks and green spaces that highlight this great place on a great lake. The first field trip stop was one of these wonderful spaces, the Urban Ecology Center. This organization, which consists of three separate locations in the heart of the city, aims to connect people in urban areas to nature and each other. Visits there with my family are always enjoyable, so the field trip would certainly kick off spectacularly. Next the group went to the aforementioned Schlitz Audubon Nature Center and Preschool. I'm biased, but I feel that this place belongs in the hall of fame of nature centers and nature preschools. I must admit I felt completely out of my league being included in this field trip, considering the significance of the other destinations. My site didn't compare to theirs in terms of diversity, flora and fauna, or sheer space. My experience and expertise couldn't hold a candle to the presenters and coordinators of those other sites. But my site did have something the others didn't: student tour guides. Wanting to differentiate the experience for the guests and always looking for ways to involve my students, I invited a handful of recently graduated nature kindergarteners to show off the trail in their own words and actions. They didn't disappoint.

But as the bus pulled up and the guests made their way to the oak tree classroom, both the student tour guides and trail were overshadowed by a family of opossums. Earlier that day while preparing our space, I'd noticed them taking refuge from the August heat by shacking up in one of our small storage boxes. I hadn't planned to highlight the opossums, but when the approximately fifty nature-loving educators from around the world arrived, the first words out of my mouth were about the opossum family. You can probably guess what happened next. The presentation shifted from introducing the trail to taking selfies with opossums. Not the start I had envisioned, but pretty typical for my classroom. What I plan and expect is never, ever as meaningful and engaging as what Mother Nature spontaneously presents. Once everyone had their fill of opossums, I gave a brief background on my story and the development of the trail. In that overview, I shared a few of the earliest emails regarding the program that I had sent, to Patti and Eliza. I know reading emails doesn't sound too riveting, but there was a method to my madness—two of the attendees *were* Patti and Eliza. They had traveled across the country, and now they were here. At Woodside Elementary. In Sussex, Wisconsin. On the Timberwolf Trail. The trail that would not have existed without them. These two influential women were physically present at the outdoor classroom they helped become a reality. This was a dream come true.

A true full circle.

The Future Is Ours

In the spring of 2020, I was separated from my students and my school family. Not by choice. The coronavirus changed every-thing. If I honestly described how this pandemic made me feel, it might look like this: "*$#@ &*% #!&^". I haven't cursed in front of my students yet (at least not out loud). As much as they can drive me crazy, being away from my students breaks my heart. The timing of this separation couldn't have been worse for a nature kindergarten class. Spring is when everything we have worked toward comes together and we practically live outside. Planting. Birding. Playing. Thriving. While away from my students, I used the time to enjoy nature adventures with my own three children. Though these adventures filled me with joy, I also yearned for my students. Teachers will understand this. Every class owns a piece of our hearts. This pan-demic created a void that nothing will ever really be able to fill. Being unable to share all the amazing nature experiences that I'd had planned with my class nearly destroyed me.

But I found an antidote to the separation pains caused by the pandemic. My prescription is nature. It dulls the symptoms and remedies the ailment of isolation from school. When I am not parked in front of a screen creating virtual lessons, meeting colleagues online, researching innovative technologies, or teaching class virtually, I get outside. I miss school. But no matter how long we are away from our school communities, at least we have nature.

Even when school reopened for the 2020–21 school year and my students and I could again be together in our classroom, things were different. Our field trips were virtual. We still met with nature friends like Mr. Stokes, our local Ice Age Trail chapter, and the International Crane Foundation, but only online or via recordings. We created a successful and unique virtual naturalist buddy project with our Retzer Nature Center friends, but it wasn't the same as meeting in person. Still, different doesn't necessarily mean worse. This new experience gave our students alternative ways to engage with nature experts. For us teachers, this new challenge stretched our creative muscles and forced us to think even further outside the box. We still valued our nature-infused philosophy and wanted to give our students that type of experience, even in a pandemic. So we did. Even when life throws you curveball after curveball, nature is there.

Now more than ever, we need to seize our time in nature. Now more than ever, we need to play. Now more than ever, we need to look past academic standards and assessments and focus on what truly matters.

Many might think what matters is getting back to "normal" as quickly as possible. However, I think we must stop putting the needs of the curriculum ahead of the needs of the children and families we serve. Most people are familiar with the so-called summer slide, when academic growth slips a little during summer. But I ask, does actual learning slide? Or is it just our assessment scores? I tend to put less stock in the slide, considering it is directly connected to assessments rather than actual learning and experiences.

Do these slides influence my opinion on how quickly we need to get right back to what we were doing pre-pandemic? Is it imperative that we play academic catch-up as quickly as possible? Absolutely not. Even though we may be facing a larger "pandemic slide," focusing on outcomes is not the answer in itself. Children are resilient if we allow them to be through support and encouragement. I am well prepared for my first set of post-pandemic students be a bit "behind" compared to the academic achievements of their predecessors. And if virtual learning is to continue on a more regular basis, I must be prepared to change my expectations for incoming students beyond just the next school year. Honestly, pandemic or not, I think we ought to change what we expect of children anyway.

Now more than ever.

Slow Down to Catch Up

"Our kids are falling behind."

"They'll never be able to catch up."

When I hear people utter phrases similar to these, many questions come to my mind:

- When did education become a race?

- Who's racing?

- How do you win the race?

- What's the prize?

- What happens if you lose?

Unfairly, this race puts more and more academic pressure on younger and younger children. Unfortunately, this race pits schools and districts against one another. This race pits teachers against one another. This race pits students against one another. Unintentionally, this race convinces families and communities that memorizing and regurgitating information supersedes a love of learning and joy in discovery. Ultimately, this race has no winners. And sadly, it doesn't seem to have an end.

Some feel that catching up means speeding up. But increasing our speed only magnifies the problems inherent in this race. To catch up, we need to slow down. Slowing down encourages relationships. Slowing down promotes inquiry. Slowing down deepens comprehension. Slowing down strengthens connections. Slowing down will catch everyone up.

So how do we slow down?

First, we change our lens by realizing our job isn't to teach students, but to teach children. That perhaps sounds odd, but it's a crucial distinction. Love first—teach second. I first heard this expression from Jed Dearybury at a play conference and it stuck with me. It makes total sense. Before we can reasonably expect our students to give the effort and energy needed to reach their maximum potential, we need to show them that we care. Mutual trust and respect are essential to forming successful working relationships between children, families, and the community. Jed and his co-author, Dr. Julie P. Jones, discuss this idea in much more detail in their book, *The Playful Classroom*.

Inserting play and infusing nature into my classroom allows me to understand each child better as an individual. I feel it also helps the children to understand themselves better. Children thrive when they feel respected and cared for. My children open up to me more than ever before because they recognize that I will put their health and happiness above everything else in our relationship. I extend this trust to their families as well. My open-door policy welcomes them anytime and every time. While I encourage them to participate in classroom activities, the real strength of our relationship is open communication. Collaboratively, we work tirelessly to build relationships that put the children first.

After we build solid relationships, we maintain them by pumping the brakes on academics and increasing social and emotional learning opportunities. Too often the quantity of academics and the competitive pressure to achieve overwhelms students, teachers, and families. A targeted implementation of social and emotional learning protects everyone's mental well-being.

Many schools plan fun icebreaker activities for the first few days of school. Sadly, once academic instruction begins, many of these more social team-building opportunities go away. Some people have the idea that students in my class play all day. What once embarrassed me now instills pride: we do play, both inside and outside. And while some consider play a waste of time, I argue that it actually saves time. Because my children play, they problem solve. Because my children play, they show resiliency. Because my children play, they express creativity. My children gain experience and strengthen skills that are crucial to academic achievement simply by playing.

Lastly, let the kids lead. Giving up control can be challenging. It's time to make the educational system fit the needs and interests of the child rather than trying to force the child into the system's constraints. In my classroom, I allow children some control over their work. For example, in my writing workshop, we have mini lessons on a particular skill, such as inserting lowercase letters or using spaces between words. During the actual writing time, the students are in charge more often than not. While I encourage and remind them about the current focus skill, they can apply it how they like. Maybe they'll write about their families. Maybe they'll write about recess. Maybe they'll write about a penguin riding a roller coaster made of candy. It doesn't matter to me as long as they're writing. Similarly, in art projects I am usually lenient with materials and celebrate unique color choices. Maybe their fall tree has blue and pink leaves. Maybe their gingerbread man is polka-dotted. Maybe their valentine heart is green. When I offer a variety of bird sheets for the class to color during our birding unit, children often go against the grain by producing orange blue jays or striped cardinals. While not accurate, the bird collage that comes from these creations is always breathtaking. I am not bound by the requirement to be regular or the need to be normal. Allowing children to freely communicate and express themselves in ways that might go against some rules can actually enhance their educational experience.

By focusing on relationships, pumping the brakes on academics, and giving more control to children, we can catch up by slowing down. Teachers and parents may read this and feel that slowing down will make reaching the high academic expectations we place on children impossible. I refute that. I personally feel that the whole system should focus on decreasing academic expectations in general, or at a minimum, changing the requirements used to meet these standards. My students are able to reach and even exceed the expectations placed in front of them, even as we dedicate so much time to emergent play and discovery in our indoor and outdoor settings.

But how?

Because we slow down. Slowing down prioritizes quality over quantity. My students don't lose any academic ground. Sure, analyzing raw data might show that fewer students reach a certain reading level, or they write fewer sentences than students of classes I taught more traditionally. But I say again, just because students can doesn't mean they should. Does my class spend the same number of minutes as others do in traditional literacy or math lessons? Probably not. Does my class spend large chunks of time playing independent of teacher instruction and guidance? Yes. Do my students leave my classroom with a well-rounded education and a wide and deep set of skills critical to building independence? I think so. Since my transformation began, students leave my classroom with more than academic scores and skills. They leave with a love of learning, a sense of stewardship, and a deeper connection to the community.

And even though we slow down, we aren't getting left behind our peers in more traditional classrooms. Just look at the data. For one thing, my students don't seem to miss school due to illness as much as they did in the past. Is it because of our switch to a play and nature-infused classroom? Answering that may create a chicken or egg situation. Does more time in nature improve their physical health, or does their interest in a more playful and child-led classroom motivate them to be there? While I can't say for sure, their assessment scores are right where they are expected to be, and their experiences are meaningful and memorable. They're not falling behind. Because they're already much further ahead, there's no need to catch up.

Flip the *But* . . .

I'd love to take my class outside

> . . . *but* I am not outdoorsy.

> . . . *but* I don't have enough time.

> . . . *but* I don't have much green space.

I'd love to add more play

> . . . *but* I don't think my administrator would allow it.

> . . . *but* I have some behavior issues in my class.

> . . . *but* I have students with additional support needs.

It's easy to challenge change with a *but*. If you think you can't, you're right. Maintaining the status quo is easy. Pardon the homophone, but *buts* are like butts—everyone has them and they all stink. So how do you overcome the *buts* that impede progress and destroy innovation? Every situation is different, so no single solution exists. However, a few things are worth considering.

I am privileged to work in a school with a healthy amount of resources. I am fortunate to have administrative and community support. I am lucky to have a wonderful green space adjacent to my school. I understand that this is certainly not the case for every teacher and parent reading this. If you are one of those teachers or parents, don't walk away dejected, claiming *but* after *but*.

All students enter the classroom with a unique set of challenges and obstacles, seen and unseen. Teachers must focus on building relationships of trust and respect with students. We must also be flexible and adaptable so we can meet the child where they are and support their further development. Admittedly, this is easier said than done. Teaching is like gardening. Each spring my family prepares our home garden and plants a variety of vegetables, which we nurture through monitoring, watering, and weeding. Some plants thrive, while others need a little extra support. Despite our best efforts, circumstances beyond our control interfere with the plants' progress, and our harvest often isn't exactly what we had hoped for at the beginning of the season. Likewise, at school each fall, the teacher prepares their classroom, then carefully nurtures and assists children who learn at different rates and in different ways. There are elements the teacher cannot control. There are elements the student cannot control. These elements can make the process of learning more challenging but never impossible.

Regardless of academic level, behavioral development, or social and emotional needs, all students should have access to what they need for health and happiness. I argue that play and nature are two of those needs. I'd go even further and state unequivocally that access to play and nature are a right for students. Every day. Every student. Regular education students. Students with additional support needs. Students of color. Private school students. Public school students. Homeschool students. Preschool students. College students. Urban school students. Rural school students. Suburban school students.

All students (and all people for that matter). Everyone has the right to get outside and experience the outdoors, whether it be a concrete slab and patch of grass or a more expansive natural area. Students deserve these opportunities even if their academic work isn't quite complete. They deserve these opportunities even if their behavior is less than perfect. In fact, in my humble opinion, struggles with behaviors or academics can be a signal that not only do they deserve these opportunities, but they need them more than others do. Their health and happiness could even depend on it.

As teachers, our responsibility is to put every child in the best position to succeed, no matter what. Demands and expectations beyond our control can easily drain us and drown us in negativity and apathy if we let them. We all need to play the hand we're dealt, but we can't suffocate the art of teaching by avoiding risks. Instead, let's practice what we preach and embrace the inevitable failures we endure with an unabashed spirit of effort and enthusiasm.

As teachers, if we allow obstacles to overwhelm us . . .

if we use students as an excuse . . .

if we *but, but, but* our way out of every situation . . .

are we doing what is more constructive for the children or what is more comfortable for the school?

Challenge yourself to flip the *but*.

You might not have a huge and accessible natural space nearby . . . *but* I bet you have a tree or patch of grass or a windowsill.

You might not have unlimited time . . . *but* you can try five minutes of play a day.

Your students might have behavioral challenges . . . *but* trying something new could help them.

Your students might need extra attention . . . *but* resources exist if you're willing to look, listen, and learn.

Change might seem too difficult or challenging . . . *but* effort eclipses execution.

You might feel inexperienced or incapable . . . *but* it isn't about you. It's about them.

If you really want to make a change, you'll figure out a way. Otherwise, an easy excuse will be waiting for you. Don't let excuses impede improvement. Stand up. Be brave. Flip the *buts*!

Plea for Passion

Growing up, I had many passions. If you haven't figured it out yet, nature is at the top of the list. Here's the rest. Every Saturday night, I desperately tried (and usually failed) to stay up late enough to watch wrestling. (It's scripted, not fake—there's a big difference.) I also spent hours sorting and organizing my baseball card collection. While I still have some cards left, I have given many of them to my students. Looking at those cards from the '80s and early '90s with their glorious facial-hair styles is always a blast. I also collected comics. Not Spiderman or Superman or any other superhero—I spent hours at discount bookstores looking for paperback books showcasing characters from newspaper comic strips. With *Beetle Bailey*, *Family Circus*, *Hagar the Horrible*, and *Calvin and Hobbes*, my collection of books spanned into the thousands. I still get a lot of kicks out of reading through and connecting to these characters. In my adolescence, I dabbled in writing stories and poetry. Now approaching my forties, I still find myself mesmerized by the world of writing. My list of picture book drafts is only bested by an even more ridiculous list of ideas that I hope to get down on paper or screen someday. And all through my childhood, my passion for sports was limitless. Being a homer, I followed my Brewers, Bucks, Packers, and Badgers religiously. Still a huge fan today, I'm always excited and anxious that this could be the year my team wins it all.

Passions don't just fade away. They follow you. They influence you. They describe you. They *are* you. The power of these passions is that they affect those around you, hopefully positively. I know I bring my passions to my personal life. Watching wrestling remains a regular event in my house. My baseball card collection, though whittled down to essentially a shoebox, still holds a place in my house, along with a stack of comic-strip paperbacks cut down from thousands to a dozen or so, since I couldn't bear to get rid of them all. While my writing samples don't take up much physical space, they certainly fill up USB flash drives. Picture book read-alouds are commonplace at any time in any room. My love for local sports teams takes up most of my TV time and most of my closet space, but the highlight is the storage shelf in my basement man-cave-turned-playroom, featuring a baseball signed by Hank Aaron and loads of mementos and memorabilia. The crown jewel might be my complete set of racing sausage bobbleheads. Needless to say, I haven't lost any of these childhood passions. They're out in the open. Why hide them when you can share them?

I especially love sharing my passions with the students I am blessed to teach every year. Without knowing me, you could take a quick tour of my classroom and get a pretty good sense of what my passions are. There's the oversized sports flags above the sink. And the wrestling storage box holding our writing supplies. And the championship belt we use for our Math Championship activity. There's an insane number of books. And of course there's a racing sausage pennant by my teacher table. I bring my passions into both my classroom design and classroom instruction. My examples and stories often intersect with my interests. You see this clearly in the nature I've brought indoors. Our nature center is loaded with artifacts—feathers, seedpods, rocks, shells, and bones. Our ceiling features labeled photographs of local species. The interactive whiteboard we are fortunate to have usually displays a wild-animal live cam, and the attached speakers regularly send out calm nature sounds like waterfalls, gentle breezes, and song-birds. I wear my passions on my sleeve, and I share them as much as I can.

When I began my career teaching fourth grade, I was men-tored by an experienced fourth-grade teacher. Though we got along fine, he was my polar opposite. He is very organized. I am . . . decidedly not. He is eloquent and thoughtful with his words. I tend to blurt out whatever comes to mind. He always keeps the big picture in mind and stays the course. My road map to learn-ing takes detours, side roads, and endures occasional pileups.

Despite these differences, we worked well together and never had communication issues. We were and still are different, and that's okay. One spring I saw a side of him I hadn't ever really noticed before: he loves jazz music. Personally, I don't mind jazz, but I also don't understand it. He'd blare his carefree and soulful music until seconds before the kids entered the room, and then, in the blink of an eye, he was all business. But that year, I saw him intentionally insert his love and passion for jazz into his instruction. He played jazz recordings for the class. He read about it. He discussed it and taught his students about famous jazz musicians past and present. The class researched the history of this musical genre. In essence, he took his passion and put it into his practice. His curriculum was properly aligned and developmentally appropriate, and above all, it oozed passion. He became energized, and best of all, his students did too. They saw and felt his passion for jazz; then they became passionate about it too.

I love nature. He loves jazz. But you don't have to do what we did. You can blaze your own trail. In fact, you should. You might love camping. Or art. Or football. Or candy. Or sewing. Or coding. Or weather. Or running. Or engineering. Or history. Or video games. Or cooking. Or fishing. Or stamp collecting. Whatever it may be, take your love and run with it. Plan a special unit. Decorate a corner of your classroom. Intentionally insert it into your instruction. Purposefully practice your passion. You won't be disappointed. Neither will your students.

Outrage into Opportunity

Meetings about meetings. Overassessing children. An unwarranted and unnecessary push for higher expectations at earlier ages. Developmentally inappropriate curricular responsibilities. Funding issues. Lack of access to technology or other resources. The diminishing or outright elimination of a child's right to the arts and recess. There are plenty of issues in the world of education today that should upset and even outrage people in and out of the profession. But far too often that indignation goes hand in hand with inaction. Being outraged and frustrated is one thing, but doing something about it? Well, that's a whole different animal. Parents may feel powerless. Besides, what could one parent in one school do? Teachers may feel overwhelmed. With so much to do already, why rock the boat and face potential backlash?

Simple—because that's what students need. And if we aren't in it for the children, we shouldn't be in it at all.

So what can we do? By we, I mean parents, teachers, administrators, community stakeholders, and most important of all, students. Individually, we can think outside the box, but collectively, we can obliterate it. It's time to speak up about what needs to change. It's time to question things we know aren't productive or positive for students and families. It's time to stand up against what is unnecessary and overappreciated. It's time to put students ahead of statistics. It's time to take that outrage and turn it into opportunity.

Parents, speak up. Though teachers want what's best for children, we often feel confined or confused by what our job requires. But we're willing to listen. Find a teacher in your school who will chat. I guarantee they'll be excited to hear a parent's perspective about making changes, whether about going outside, the power of play, or some other passion. But most importantly, we must work together to get the ball rolling to make change happen. If you can't find a teacher to get started, connect with an administrator. Or take a more active role in a parent-teacher organization. Find other like-minded parents. You may feel like no one is listening, but if you don't say anything, there is zero chance you will be heard. Never stop prodding.

Teachers, speak up. You know what is best for kids, yet you also know that some of what you are required to do doesn't fit that description. Do your research. Be ready to share personal examples. Want to go outside? Research. Want to play more? Research. Decision makers love data. Data seems to run the world these days, so you might as well use it to your advantage. Connect with other teachers. Listen to your families. Listen to your students. Listen to your heart. Be willing to change what you do, even if it ruffles feathers. Never stop pushing.

Administrators, speak up. Your school might need a shake-up. You might feel and see stress in students, teachers, and families. You're not alone. Listen to your staff. Embrace innovative and risky approaches. Allow flexibility and freedom in your classrooms. Let the passion and art of teaching drive your school. Believe and trust that teachers will do what's best for their children by doing what's best for all the teachers. Be firm and fair. Set an example of passion for your staff, students, and families. Never stop pressing.

Community stakeholders, speak up. Reach out to schools. Learn what they are doing, and more importantly, find out what they need. Learn how you can get involved. Education takes a group effort. And funding. Using your time, talent, and treasure will pay off now and in the future. Community collaborations set up schools and students for success. Never stop participating.

Students, speak up! Talk to your parents. Talk to your teachers. Talk to your administrators. Be active in your community. Speak up for what you believe in. Share what you need. Understand that risk is necessary and that not everything is easy. Appreciate the f-word—failure promotes growth. As cliché as it sounds, you are the future, so you might as well personally invest yourself in getting there. Trust your parents. Trust your teachers. Above all, trust yourself. Listen more than you speak, but definitely don't be silent. And regardless of anything you hear from anyone else, take this last piece of advice to heart. Never stop playing!

Afterword
Tales
from the Trail

Teaching Off Trail is about storytelling. Hopefully these stories were engaging and inspiring. Because every classroom has their own stories to tell, I couldn't think of a better way to wrap up this book of stories than by sharing some quotes, anecdotes, and activities pulled directly from our classroom. These stories provide another glimpse into my reasoning and rationale for my need to go off trail and stay there.

My Favorite Child and Family Quotes

"I like to climb fallen trees. I was scared the first time I tried it, but then I got really good at it!"

"I loved doing *Cookies for a Cause* and other things [to raise money] for Children's Wisconsin. They use the money to help other kids feel better, and that makes me feel happy."

"Playing in my classroom was fun. I liked dressing up and doing art with my friends. Playing on the trail was even better. Finding a toad was my favorite."

"Play at school is important because you can use your curiosity to learn stuff."

"The best part of playing on the trail is finding animals and bugs. A bumblebee kissed my hand one time, and now I love bumblebees."

"Playing and being outside let you be in your own world and control your own imagination."

"Being outside helped me be me. I got to play with my friends, get exercise, take care of my energy, and have fun. And now when I go outside, I can teach my family and make my world healthy."

"Knowing my child would be outside a lot was nerve-wracking, but seeing the joy in his eyes when he talked about school made up for the nerves. He is able to read and do math just as well as other kids, and he connects with nature. It is a bonus."

"To hear five-year-olds talk about what a conifer is and understand it really showed the engagement of the kids. And they talk about basic nature safety, like how to protect from ticks. The five-year-olds also get to decide what to wear to prepare for nature class that day. Their passion for nature comes through when we hear about what happened at school that day."

"My child has a tendency to be very shy around others and lacks confidence when trying new things. I think nature kindergarten has shown her that interacting with other students is fun and has helped her have more confidence in herself as a student and friend."

"My child sits at the window every morning in silence, looking for birds. The silence ends when she sees one, especially one she hasn't taught us about yet."

"My daughter always enjoyed being outdoors, but has gained a greater love for it now that she's a 'nature kindergartner' (as she calls herself when bragging). She gets very excited to see what they'll find on the trail camera. When we visit parks, family, and so forth, she tells anyone and everyone all about the outdoors. She also pulls any garlic mustard she finds, and explains why she has to pull it (sometimes the adults don't even know what it is). She has learned many things that her older siblings do not know, which is very empowering to her. She now has asked to be in charge of our garden at home."

"My son's passion for nature and how things work is amazing. He has gained so much knowledge. He has such a profound level of respect for nature, as all of the children in the classroom seem to. You can see it in their faces and in their eyes. They light up when they are able to make the connections between what Mr. Dargatz read to them or taught them and then seeing it happen right in front of them outside. When my son comes home from school, as tired as he may be, he still pushes himself to get outside, and he recognizes that it really makes him feel better."

"I love the story you shared on the Nature Kindergarten Family night about the girl who was ready for first grade academically but you felt that you didn't help her socially. That really resonated with me and is a great reason *why* you do what you do. I absolutely love that the kids were encouraged to use their imaginations, their problem-solving skills, and a lot of leadership skills as well."

"I've learned to sit back and observe them in play more. Even with his younger sister, he has been more open to working with her and almost teaching her while they play rather than directing her and bossing her around. He loves play days and doesn't even realize all the skills he's gaining."

Be a Flower

She was a girly girl, wearing beautiful dresses every day with matching accessories. Her footwear wasn't always suitable for outdoor exploration, but she never complained. One September morning early in her kindergarten career, she stood peacefully by the field of goldenrod, flower dress and all. When a buzzing bee took interest in the flower design of her dress, she was anything but peaceful. As I heard her scream and saw her swats, I took advantage of this teachable moment. I gave her simple advice and asked her to be like a flower and stand still. I calmly informed her that the bee was just doing what bees do, looking for a flower to gather nectar from. If she stood still, the bee would realize her flowers were nectar-free and search somewhere else, but if she screamed and flailed, the bee would protect itself by stinging. She heeded my advice and escaped the situation sting-free. As the year developed, she encountered other risks with confidence. By the end of the year, she became a huge nature advocate and got down and dirty in the mud as much as anyone else, flower dress and all.

Chipmunk Prognostication

Some people seem to think the groundhog can predict the future. There's even a holiday in honor of this belief. But in my experience, I think this honor and privilege should instead be bestowed upon the groundhog's smaller cousin, the chipmunk.

On one of the first days of nature kindergarten, I noticed a small group of children huddled together on the trail. As I approached, I realized that what had brought them together was a chipmunk whose day of reckoning had come. Listening to them talk, I was surprised to hear that the buzz around their discovery was intrigue, not disgust. I decided this was a perfect opportunity to teach with chain questioning, a technique used to further exploration through asking questions instead of answering them. The students had plenty to say. Here is a paraphrased overview of our conversation.

Student: What happened to the chipmunk?

Me: Not sure. What do you think happened?

Student: He broke his leg.

Me: Why do you say that?

Student: Because chipmunks are fast, so he should've gotten away.

Me: So, if a chipmunk breaks his leg, he will die?

Student: Yep.

Me: People break their bones all the time and they don't die. Why is it different for a chipmunk?

Student: Because they don't go to the doctor.

Me: Well, if there aren't any chipmunk doctors, how do they take care of themselves?

Student: They hide. They are super speedy.

Me: And if their leg is broken, they aren't super speedy anymore and it's harder for them to hide, right?

Student: Yeah. They'd get eaten.

Me: Great thought! But, if that's correct, how come this chipmunk hasn't been eaten?

A pause for some much-needed thought.

Me: Let's take a closer look and see if there are any clues.

Student: There's a hole in his neck.

Me: You're right. What could that mean?

Student: The hole is bloody, so it must have run into something sharp, like a rock.

Me: Possibly. That would have to be one very sharp rock. Does anyone else have any other ideas?

Student: Maybe it's one of the hawks we saw last week.

At this point, I had a hard time holding in my excitement. Luckily, the students took over the conversation, so I didn't need to.

Student 1: Yeah, the hawk has sharp nails and loves to eat mice.

Student 2: Why didn't the hawk eat it?

Student 1: Maybe the hawk dropped it and couldn't find it.

Student 2: Or maybe a loud noise scared it off.

This chipmunk forecasted some of the wonderful positives of nature kindergarten, including creativity, collaboration, critical thinking, and communication.

"Hey, Little Buddy"

Most students take to nature kindergarten in an instant. Some warm up over time. Occasionally a few just aren't into it. This particular student fell into that third category. Regardless of activity, weather, or topic, he tended to avoid doing much of anything in our outdoor classroom. His behaviors and actions weren't much different inside. He tended to stay guarded. I knew he had trust issues related to his family situation and usually avoided getting too close to adults. I respected that but also wanted to see if I could build from his past experiences to positively influence his future. However, I failed, no matter how I tried, and the divide between us grew daily. I never gave up, but I often felt helpless. Then Mother Nature jumped in.

As he typically spent much of his outside time at a safe distance from his peers, I took notice one day when I saw him working closely with a few other classmates. When I got there, I saw that he was talking, but not to the other students. On his forearm sat a tiny praying mantis. The sharp, distant tone of his voice melted away as he talked to this unique insect that had hitched a ride on his arm. We chatted a little bit, but I could tell he wanted some time with his new friend. I gave him space, but stayed close enough to observe and listen. He talked to this mantis as if they were long-lost friends. And as he told the insect about Legos, Star Wars, fruit snacks, and hunting, he began every sentence with, "Hey, little buddy."

As the end of the day drew near, I became concerned about how he might react. Would he beg to keep his new friend? Would he get sad or mad about leaving the mantis behind? Would some of his challenging behaviors worsen? Wrong on all counts.

When the time came to head inside and get ready to go home, he gently placed the praying mantis on a leaf. I heard him say one thing as he walked away: "Hey, little buddy. Great talking to you. Hope to see you again."

Me too, little buddy. Me too.

Skulls, Skulls Everywhere

Every year there's at least one student who seems unusually adept at finding things. One year it was a young girl who always found morel mushrooms. Another year, no matter where he went or what he did, one boy always found a tick, or maybe the ticks found him. And once I had a student who found skulls. Everywhere.

The first find was a great discovery. The second skull was just plain luck. By the sixth or seventh skull, I started to wonder how he did it. He'd gotten so good at discovering skulls that he'd found some in his own neighborhood, to the cautious delight of his mother. While she appreciated his newfound skill and took joy in his excitement, she made sure to suggest adding "nature gloves" to the following year's school supply list.

One day he upped his skull-finding game by discovering an entire raccoon carcass. Seeing this as a wonderful teaching opportunity, I sectioned off a small area around the raccoon so we could witness the process of decomposition.

Over the next few weeks, we noticed how the raccoon changed, the flies increased, and the smell worsened. But in the name of fun and learning, we kept watching. Someone or something else must have been watching as well.

Checking the carcass had become routine, so the students were taken aback when they noticed one day that its skull had disappeared. Our skull sleuths began investigating. The case soon wrapped up as quickly as it had begun when our skull expert came through once again with another find. However, the skull wasn't alone—he also found a feather. A big one.

He asked to bring the class together so he could report on his findings. I obliged. When the class convened, he told an elaborate tale full of appropriate and logical nature information. He concluded that a turkey vulture had moved the skull away from the rest of the body so the bird could enjoy the skull without interference. He said the bird was probably picking the skull clean when something startled it, causing it to fly off without the skull and lose a feather in the process.

We may never know the actual sequence of events, and quite frankly, I don't even care. The joy of nature kindergarten is not in the destination but in the journey. Based on the enthusiasm with which this student shared his turkey vulture theory, he'd had quite an incredible journey.

Walk with a Hawk

Assessment weeks are always our least favorite weeks of the year. As exhausting as it is for the teacher to give all the required assessments, it is much more tedious for a kindergartener to take them, so during this week, we take advantage of every free moment to rejuvenate our bodies and minds outside.

We wrapped up one mild winter day by heading out to the trail. After a full day of number crunching and data collecting, we'd certainly needed it. While most kids were climbing trees and enjoying the snow, one gentleman stayed a little behind with his eyes to the skies. He had noticed something.

With a smile a mile wide, he called me over and told me about a solitary hawk stoically settled on the top of a bare oak tree. Another boy overheard and ventured over. Within seconds of spotting the majestic bird, it took off and soared to another tree a few hundred feet away. The walk with a hawk had begun. For the remainder of our time outside, these two boys followed their new hawk friend around. Seeing the bird soar was impressive. But not nearly as awe-inspiring as watching the boys light up as they followed it around. This is the kind of moment that makes the data collection bearable. This is the magic of taking kids outside.

You Don't Have to Take My Word for It

Growing up, I loved watching *Reading Rainbow*, an educational program dedicated to reading. And I still do. My favorite episode, titled "How Much is a Million?," could possibly be the best twenty-seven minutes in American television history. Not exaggerating at all. This episode features host LeVar Burton visiting a crayon factory to learn how crayons are made. Watching crayon after crayon work its way through the machines on its journey to join a box of perfectly organized and shaped crayons is pure magic. That episode might also be the reason I asked my dad every year to buy me two new crayon boxes—one to use and one to admire. But I digress.

A special part of that show highlights a few children's books related to the topic at hand. Before children talk about each book, Burton says, "You don't have to take my word for it." In my journey, I've found amazing resources, read inspirational books, and met the greatest group of individuals who put children first. If I've failed to convince you that following your passion and going off trail will work for you, maybe these resources can. So bear with me as I summon my best LeVar Burton imitation: You don't have to take my word for it.

Moving the Classroom Outdoors: Schoolyard-Enhanced Learning in Action by Herbert Broda

Play: How It Shapes the Brain, Opens the Imagination, and Invigorates the Soul by Stuart Brown and Christopher Vaughan

The Playful Classroom: The Power of Play for All Ages by Jed Dearybury and Julie P. Jones

The Power of Play: Learning What Comes Naturally by David Elkind

Free to Learn: Why Unleashing the Instinct to Play Will Make Our Children Happier, More Self-Reliant, and Better Students for Life by Peter Gray

Balanced and Barefoot: How Unrestricted Outdoor Play Makes for Strong, Confident, and Capable Children by Angela Hanscom

Preschool beyond Walls: Blending Early Childhood Education and Nature-Based Learning by Rachel Larimore

Last Child in the Woods: Saving Our Children from Nature-Deficit Disorder by Richard Louv

A Forest Days Handbook: Program Design for School Days Outside by Eliza Minnucci with Meghan Turnout

Lisa Murphy on Being Child Centered by Lisa Murphy

Nature-Based Preschool Professional Practice Guidebook by North American Association for Environmental Education, edited by Christy Merrick

Nature-Based Learning for Young Children: Anytime, Anywhere, on Any Budget by Julie Powers and Sheila Williams Ridge

Let the Children Play: How More Play Will Save Our Schools and Help Children Thrive by Pasi Sahlberg and William Doyle

How to Raise a Wild Child: The Art and Science of Falling in Love with Nature by Scott D. Sampson

Nature Preschools and Forest Kindergartens: The Handbook for Outdoor Learning by David Sobel

The Sky Above and the Mud Below: Lessons from Nature Preschools and Forest Kindergartens by David Sobel

The Power of Place: Authentic Learning through Place-Based Education by Tom Vander Ark, Emily Liebtag, and Nate McClennen

Play at the Center of the Curriculum by Judith VanHoorn, Patricia Nourot, Barbara Scales, and Keith Alward

Nature Play Workshop for Families: A Guide to 40+ Outdoor Learning Experiences in All Seasons by Monica Wiedel-Lubinski and Karen Madigan

Children & Nature Network: www.childrenandnature.org

Field Edventures: www.fieldedventures.org

Inside-Outside, Nature-Based Educators: www.insideoutside.org

Natural Start Alliance: https://naturalstart.org

Teaching Off Trail: peterdargatz.com

References

Akhtar, Zaiba, Erah Ali, Kaitlyn M. Constantino, and Azhar Hussain. 2018. "The Effects of Play-Based Learning on Early Childhood Education and Development." *Journal of Evolution of Medical and Dental Sciences.* 7, no. 43. https://doi.org/10.14260/jemds/2018/1044.

Bailie, Patti Ensel, PhD. 2014. "Forest School in Public School: Is It Possible?" Natural Start Alliance. https://naturalstart.org/feature-stories /forest-school-public-school-it-possible#.

Bradbury, Alice, and Guy Roberts-Holmes. 2016. "The Datafication of Early Years Education and Its Impact upon Pedagogy." *Improving Schools* 19, no. 2:119–28. https://doi.org/10.1177/1365480216651519.

Brown, Stuart, and Christopher Vaughan. 2009. *Play: How It Shapes the Brain, Opens the Imagination, and Invigorates the Soul.* New York: Penguin Random House.

Clark, Alexander, Nicholas Holt, Homan Lee, Linda Slater, John Spence, and Katherine Tamminen. 2015. "A Meta-Study of Qualitative Research Examining Determinants of Children's Independent Active Free Play." *International Journal of Behavioral Nutrition and Physical Activity* 12, no. 5. https://doi.org/10.1186/s12966-015-0165-9.

Dearybury, Jed, and Julie P. Jones. 2020. *The Playful Classroom: The Power of Play for All Ages.* Hoboken, NJ: Jossey-Bass.

Delzer, Kayla. 2016. "Flexible Seating and Student-Centered Classroom Redesign." Edutopia. https://www.edutopia.org/blog /flexible-seating-student-centered-classroom-kayla-delzer.

Doyle, William, and Pasi Sahlberg. 2019. *Let the Children Play: How More Play Will Save Our Schools and Help Children Thrive.* Oxford: Oxford University Press.

Elkind, David. 2007. *The Power of Play: Learning What Comes Naturally.* Boston: Da Capo Press.

Fisher, Kelly R., Roberta M. Golinkoff, Kathy Hirsh-Pasek, and Nora Newcombe. 2013. "Taking Shape: Supporting Preschoolers' Acquisition of Geometric Knowledge through Guided Play." *Child Development* 84, no. 6: 1872–78.

Gray, Peter. 2013. *Free to Learn: Why Unleashing the Instinct to Play Will Make Our Children Happier, More Self-Reliant, and Better Students for Life.* New York: Basic Books.

Gull, Carla, Suzanne Levenson Goldstein, and Tricia Rosengarten. 2016. "Benefits and Risks of Tree Climbing on Child Development and Resiliency." *International Journal of Early Childhood Environmental Education* 5, no. 2: p. 10.

Harmon, Flora, and Radhika Viruru. 2018. "Debunking the Myth of the Efficacy of "Push-Down Academics": How Rigid, Teacher-Centered, Academic Early Learning Environments Dis-Empower Young Children." *Journal of Family Strengths* 18, no. 1: art. 11. https://digitalcommons.library.tmc.edu/jfs/vol18/iss1/11.

Hutchings, Merryn. 2015. *Exam Factories? The Impact of Accountability Measures on Children and Young People.* National Union of Teachers. https://www.basw.co.uk/system/files/resources/basw_112157-4_0.pdf.

Jordan, Ijumaa. 2016. "Ijumaa, Why Is Play an Equity Issue?" Diversity & Equity Education for Adults, NAEYC Interest Forum. https://earlychildhoodequity.wordpress.com/2016/02/10/ijumaa-why-is-play-an-equity-issue/.

Kohn, Alfie. 2006. *The Homework Myth: Why Our Kids Get Too Much of a Bad Thing.* New York: Hachette.

Miller, Edward, and Joan Almon. 2009. *Crisis in the Kindergarten: Why Children Need to Play in School.* College Park, MD: Alliance for Childhood. https://files.eric.ed.gov/fulltext/ED504839.pdf.

Murphy, Lisa. 2016. *Lisa Murphy on Play: The Foundation of Children's Learning.* St. Paul, MN: Redleaf Press.

North American Association for Environmental Education, and Christy Merrick, ed. 2019. *Nature-Based Preschool Professional Practice Guidebook: Teaching, Environments, Safety, Administration.* Washington, DC: North American Association for Environmental Education.

Pham, Lam D., Tuan D. Nguyen, and Matthew G. Springer. 2020. "Teacher Merit Pay: A Meta-Analysis." *American Educational Research Journal.* https://doi.org/10.3102/0002831220905580.

Silverman, Sarah K. 2019. *Taking Back Kindergarten: Rethinking Rigor for Young Learners.* Teaching Strategies. https://teachingstrategies.com/wp-content/uploads/2019/10/Taking_Back_Kindergarten_Teaching_Strategies_2019.pdf.

Index